D1192464

simply droog

simply
droog

simply droog

simply droog

simply droog

simply droog

10 + 3 years of creating
innovation and discussion

simply droog

simply droog

intro-duction

Renny Ramakers and Gijs Bakker

In April 1993 we made our debut at the International Furniture Fair in Milan. We presented sixteen products in an old villa in the city centre. A bundle of second-hand drawers, a chair made of rags, piled up lamp shades, a coffee-maker in which bicycle lamps were mounted, a bookcase made of paper... they formed a strong contrast with the chic antique cupboards and tables that the villa was furnished with. There was no information, no price lists, just the products.

It was a try-out. We had no idea how the discriminating design lover would react. We sort of felt that 'if they like it we'll go on', if not, then we'll stop. The first days were alarmingly quiet but slowly it began to buzz. And on the last day there was a roaring trade. Dealers inquired about prices. The press asked for pictures. And the leading newspaper Liberation published a favorable article: Droog Design had shown that simplicity didn't have to be boring.

Now, with the second edition of this book, to which developments occurring in 2004 and 2005 have been added, the number of products in the Droog collection has in the meantime grown to more than 200 objects. The products are very diverse. The one product is a distinct statement, the other is somewhat quieter. But all of them are dry (droog), which is to say that they are based on clear concepts carried out in an equally clear manner. Our criteria are very flexible, being led by cultural developments and by our intuition.

The activities of Droog Design have grown tremendously in the past years and are still expanding. We make exhibitions, we give lectures, we initiate experimental projects, we carry out commissions for companies and organizations, we produce and distribute products, we publish books, we supervise the IM Masters course at the Design Academy in Eindhoven and we have a shop cum gallery in Amsterdam. In 2004 we established Droog BV as a limited company, which now produces more than sixty products from the Droog collection with a lot of new products on the way.

This book was first published in 2004 to accompany the touring exhibition 'Simply Droog. 10 + 1 years of creating discussion and innovation'. The tour was kicked off on 17 May 2004 in the Haus der Kunst in Munich and afterwards travelled to the Design Zentrum in Bremen, the Gemeentemuseum in The Hague, Mudac in Lausanne and Museum Bellerive in Zürich and Museo Oscar Niemeyer in Curitiba. The reprinting of this book coincides with the updated sequel to this successful tour, taking in Grand Hornu Images in Belgium and the Museum of Arts & Design in New York.

A look back should include a word of thanks to all those who have played an important role in the past years. In particular we wish to thank all the designers we have worked with, of whom there are now more than 100. Thanks to their efforts, enthusiasm and creativity, our products have become what they are. Without the designers there would be no Droog Design!

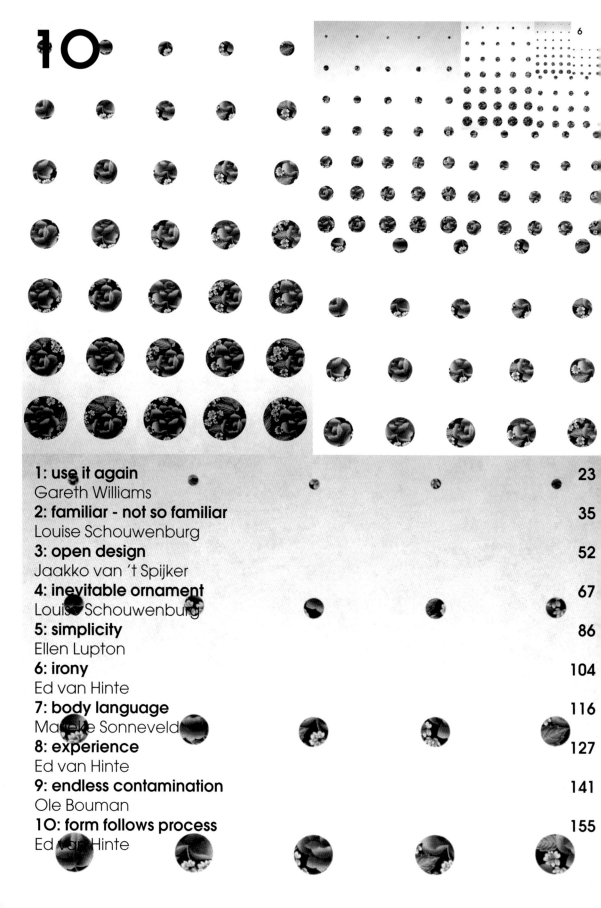

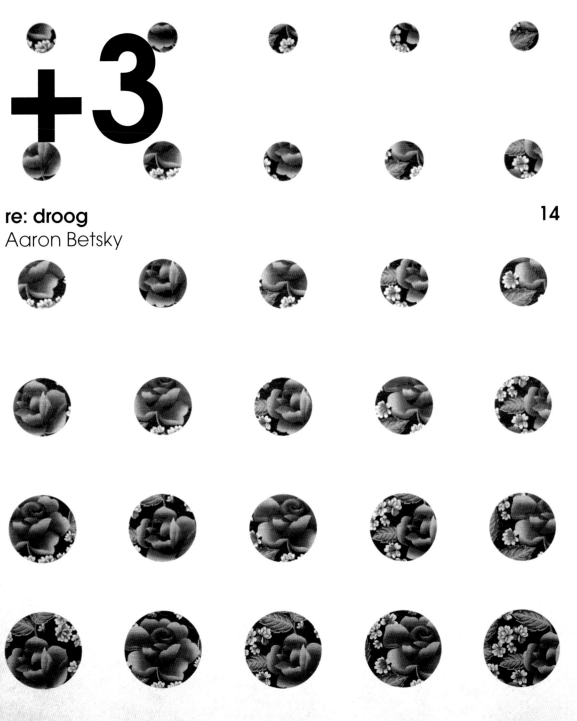

+3

re: droog
Aaron Betsky

2002: 244

2000: 221

1998: 200

1996: 181

1994: 169

1995: 1

1995: 173

1997: 185

1999: 207

2001: 232

2003: 258

2004: 278

200.
294

re: droog

Aaron Betsky

Director of the Netherlands Architecture
Institute, Rotterdam, critic and teacher.

Presentation of 'Couleur Locale' at the
1999 Salone di Mobile in Milan

There is something oddly familiar about Droog Design. Though for ten years now the
objects chosen for the collection continue to astonish, amaze and puzzle, they evoke
a warm, fuzzy feeling of deja vu. Haven't I seen that combination oil and vinegar
dispenser, that chest of drawers with its mismatched members, that chair with one
leg much too short, propped up on a stack of books, that shape of a vase – though
its material seems strange – and that children's chair? Of course I have. Droog is a
collection of the detritus of our culture, reassembled, rearranged and repurposed.
But something still remains. For those of us who, like many of the designers who produce work for the Droog Collection, grew up in 1960s and 1970s, there is something
hippie-like and thus familiar about Droog.

What brought this home to me was the 'Couleur Locale' installation presented at the
1999 Salone di Mobile in Milan. After a few years of presenting the archest, funniest,
and freshest objects at that annual confab of designers and manufacturers, Droog
Design presented a coherent project. Aimed at revitalizing the area around the former estate of an obscure Dutch princess married to a German prince in what was
for a brief but destructive period East Germany, the presentation consisted of orange

lollipops molded around orange seeds so that you could plant them to grow new trees, a log onto which backs of old chairs were stuck to make it a comfortable sitting apparatus, a nouveau cane chair and my own personal favorite, a machine into which gardeners could feed all the leaves they raked off the ground in the fall, after which the composter would spit out a bench-shaped compression of the detritus. Through the mechanism of gathering and re-shaping, they created the ability to enjoy the park's rebirth in the spring and the memory of its fall before the bench decomposed in the summer and the whole process started over again, now with a reconfigured machine producing new forms of benches. The design was clever, the purpose noble, and the presentation as seductive as ever, but what struck me was the overall sensibility: all-natural fibres, Third World (well, Second World) development aid with a fondness for the manners of the distant locale, do-it-yourself technology, and participatory design were all back, but in a new guise.

Perhaps it was the time. Ex-hippies ruled. It was the period of the Third Way, when politicians such as Bill Clinton and Gerhard Schröder were making the world better by collaborating with capitalists while misbehaving in their private lives – as were designers such as Wolf Prix and Philippe Starck. It was the years when Microsoft was using John Lennon and Apple was co-opting all the heroes of those halcyon days. At the same time, design was becoming less an elite pursuit and more of a way to, as Tom Peters said at the Aspen Design Conference the spring before the Oranienbaum presentation, 'make you filthy, stinking rich.' So it occurred to me: now that the generation of '68 has grown up and proven themselves capable of turning the revolution into a car-selling theme song while behaving as badly as possible in positions of power to prove their wild spirit, it is left to their children to rebel against their sell-out and argue for the values they left behind – sustainability, spirituality, learning from other cultures, using as little technology as possible, participatory design, politics and work, freeing your body and your mind, and wearing and eating only natural products. For all the critical rhetoric, irony and high design that characterizes Droog Design, this is perhaps their most lasting and important contribution: that they have institutionalized political and social criticism as a lifestyle – the hippie way of revolution – into design and thus into at least some small part of our daily lives.

At the core of this lifestyle is the notion of recurrence, as if the spiritual beliefs borrowed from other cultures and cults had found their way into the very core of the design profession. Just as the 1960s seemed to be coming back again, so Renny Ramakers, Gijs Bakker and their merry band of design pranksters were arguing for a design process based on re-use –not just of materials, as Ramakers was quick to point out, but of ideas and concepts as well. The core belief of Droog Design seemed to be that design was not a question of making more objects, using more materials, or even inventing new ideas or solutions to the problems we encounter in our daily lives, but one of finding more ways to experience, explore and expand the possibilities of existing objects, images, spaces and ideas. Like squatters in the history of art or the structures of mass production, they hunkered down with what they had inherited, scavenged, salvaged and maybe even stolen, turning it into communal artifacts. For that is what they did make that was new: a community. Droog is a kind of design tribe.

The precise precedents and models the members of this flock used or reacted against have already been exhaustively documented, not least by Droog itself. What is important is to point out what Droog was and is not in the world of design. It is a loose group of people who are engaged in design as a way of revealing and reassembling our reality, thus using the elements of daily life to reflect on and criticize the structures controlling that inhabited landscape. It is a way of exposing hidden structures in the blandness of what is all around us through irony, rhetoric, misuse and deformation.

Droog does not believe that design means the whittling down of the 'solution' or object so that it is the most minimal response to the 'problem.' I do not think that it even allows for the notion of problem or solution. It is, in other words, something that does not fit in the reigning ideology of our times, which is that of efficiency. Through analysis (preferably computer-based, but led by consultants), streamlining, just-in-time inventory, organizational modeling, and outsourcing, the absolutely most minimal means of producing something is achieved. This is not just a question of business practices, but is also the prevalent political and even religious mode of operation.

On the other side of the coin, Droog also does not believe in the hook, the soundbite or the brand. After the product is made, after all, it has to be sold and consumed. This is done by reducing the object, image or space (again) to the most minimal state, but in this case that is, as it is popular to say, a 'meme': a catchphrase, image or icon that is so inescapable and seductive that it embeds itself into an operating system, whether human or not, and becomes an inalienable part of that host. This is, again, the way in which all productions and systems of production present themselves in our Western culture. Branding is god, or perhaps the other way around.

All design is thus value engineered to produce a meme. It is this essence that is expressed in the work of almost every design star (itself a concept that is in part a sign of our times) and studio, and that sets the framework for almost all design discussions. It is this framework that Droog rejected, in the same way their hippie precursors rejected 'the system,' which in those days was largely a bureaucracy and a mass market. Droog did so by arguing for assembly over code, sustainability over evanescence, and provisional and collaborative identity over branding and homogenization. If, in the end, they came dangerously close to efficiently producing a brand – well, look how many records Jefferson Airplane sold in their day.

Thirdly, Droog does not present itself as a coherent actor, organization or group. It is not a person, nor is it a company in the traditional sense of the word. It thus also escapes from the continual discussion about the role of the genius creator in the making of the object, image or space of design. There are several designers who have contributed many designs to the Droog Design collection – Marcel Wanders comes to mind – who have chosen to use this particular model to market themselves and their products, but as a loosely defined whole Droog has resolutely refused to make a division between stars and supporting actors, or between creatives and suits. Nor have they developed a corporate working method in the manner of, for instance, frogdesign or IDEO, that stands in for that particular focus on personality. Droog is rather a mess that coheres only because of the enthusiasm of its participants, by the fact that, in 2000, it was given official status by the Dutch government, ensuring it a constant stream of funding, and because of the energy of its co-organizers, Renny Ramakers and Gijs Bakker.

So if Droog does not produce efficient solutions that can be quickly consumed because they are the work of creative geniuses, what are they doing? They are addressing the three central questions of our day – the reduction of all our reality to a scrim draped over codes, sustainability and identity – through a strategy of experimentation, deformation and recombination. As such, they are part of a larger movement in many fields of culture, including architecture, fine arts and even music – a fact they themselves pointed out in their most recent full self-documentation (Renny Ramakers, Less + More, 2002).

The first of these issues is the disappearance of a graspable and therefore controllable reality through the application of technology. Quite simply, the way things function, how they are made and what their purpose may be is becoming increasingly difficult to ascertain. Technology is miniaturizing the actual working of most objects beyond our ability to sense them. As we make more and use of wireless technologies, it is also dissolving operations into the ether. Standardization has developed into componization, so that even the coherence of objects is in question. The pseudo-sciences of ergonomics, human factors and market research, as well as the real science of efficient manufacturing and dense packaging, have at the same time made things more and more homogenous. Moreover, the resulting objects begin to take on the quality of human or organic beings, both to be able to fit into or with the body more readily and because we are learning the more efficient ways of nature. It is not a question of making distinct objects with which one has a clear relationship, but of camouflaging and integrating technology into every aspect of our lives.

The result is a smooth, plastic reality that is inundating more and more of what we encounter in our artificial reality. Our cars, our remote controls, our telephones, our clothes, our chairs, our contact lenses and our facades are all blending, folding and blobbing into each other. Yet this is not what we see or experience, at least not consciously. Mass produced goods and landscapes form the ground or bass, continuous and rhythmic, on which the forests of signs grow. These images clothe the media-satured stageset we inhabit with multiple scrims and screens, turning anonymous places into hot spots and pleasant abodes at the flip of a switch or the charge of a credit card. The products of mass media and our ability to image anything we can imagine, these visual fragments take the place of the variety of our tactile reality. It is how we know the world: through ephemeral images.

All of this designed Third Reality, which is replacing the first reality of nature and the second one humans made on top of that ground, is the result of codes: computer codes, chemical codes producing plastics, encryption and translation codes for wireless devices, building and safety codes, codes for engineering efficiency, codes such as typologies and language, and last but not least, codes of behavior. It is through these codes that we make and control our world and increasingly are made and controlled by it. What Droog does is quite simply to make these codes visible in themselves by messing them up. They did this most literally in the 'Bar Code' device they exhibited in 2001 at SFMOMA in San Francisco, in which the barcode on the back of any ID would activate a random response from a collection of designed devices, and in the 'do create' project of the preceding year, produced in collaboration with Amsterdam advertising agency Kessels Kramer. In most of their work, however, the issue of coding plays a prominent part. What is meant for one use is misused or shown to be something else, whether it is Hella Jongerius' experiments with rubber containers or Tejo Remy's Milk Bottle Lamp, construction (Marcel Wander's famous Rope Chair) or the ritual of use, as in much of Jurgen Bey's work. In some cases, Droog products mess with fundamental codes, though this is an attitude found more among designers who pursue their ideas inspired by, but outside the collection of, Droog (like Jan Velthuizen with his gourds 'reprogrammed' to grow into containers, or as Marti Guixe proposed doing with his 'designer drugs'). At other times, code itself, as in Joost Grooten's Braille doorhandles, becomes the subject. Quite simply, Droog makes things that ain't what they appear to be.

The ethical justification for much of this work is that it thus counters the waste of producing ever more things that use ever more energy and leave ever more waste. For the last forty years, ever since the Club of Rome released their devastating report, Limits to Growth, in 1972, we have had to confront the reality that we are depleting our natural resources at an unsustainable rate. Though this might sound like an obvious and perhaps tiring mantra, we have not been able to produce adequate responses to this overwhelming reality. It drives most of the political and social conflicts on the globe and hangs like a pall over all our activities. Lately, as we watch the Polar icecaps melt and our sea levels rise even more rapidly than predicted, even the most abstract and outrageous effects of our irresponsible actions are becoming a reality.

The traditional response in the field of design has been to produce objects, images and spaces that are completely and ironically dominated by technology. Solar collectors, hybrid materials, recyclable forms and all manner of composting toilets, recycling pumps and heat generators dominate the field of sustainable design. As such, any design that actually works in a responsible manner is experienced by most consumers as being an alien thing. Buying and then living with sustainable design is like taking an unpleasant medicine or tithing your income to a new kind of church. It is not a natural part of your everyday life. Droog has begun to effect a change in this attitude precisely by self-consciously playing with this very image. Just as many of the designers who have made Droog products and projects wear their ecological beliefs on their sleeves, so

Barcode Interpreter

design Lauran Schijvens in cooperation with Thonik and Ed van Hinte.

System Almighty. 010101 Art in Technological Times, exhibition SF MOMA, San Francisco March 3-July 8, 2001.

their designs often highlight an aesthetic of sustainability carried to a rhetorical extreme. Jurgen Bey's similar assemblies of used furniture and cloth are a perfect example of this. The dream of an 'autarchic house' in which Hella Jongerius and her husband Lucas Verweij hoped to live, was as much a showplace of sustainability as a real proposal, and resembled the Case Study program in Los Angeles in its attempts at transparency and jaunty optimism. Many of the parts of the Oranienbaum Project removed the production of new or manmade objects completely from the scope of work, reducing designers to people who can merely cultivate their garden, to paraphrase Candide.

By transforming a junkshop aesthetic into high art, and by marrying this appearance to a direct and conscious manipulation of systems of control (which is what codes, after all, represent), Droog has, by hook and by crook, produced something that comes dangerously close to a recognizable style. And indeed they need to, because in this manner they have been able to address the third issue, that of identity. The question of who one is in a world in which what one experiences with one's senses is not always what one understands to be possible in, say, quantum physics – a situation where abstract thinking and sensory knowledge have become uncoupled and con-cept and object are understood as separate –, where one understands one's very consciousness as a relative concept that may itself be the result of codes that can be manipulated, and in which one functions as a part of a global production and consumption machine, is determined as much by what one decides one's identity will be. As Anthony Giddens (Modernity and Self-indentity: Self and Society in the Late Modern Age, 1991) and Ulrich Beck (Risk Society, Towards a New Modernity, 1992) point out, the central task these days in the Western World is not just survival, but the continual construction of identity. Place, space and the scenery with which we outfit that geography are central to this process.

The result is that more and more design is aimed at providing the accoutrements for tribal associations that together perform the task of staging the kind of reality in and through our artificial environment in which its participants want to take part. Defined by allegiances to certain kinds of music, fashion brands, sports, sexual preferences, religious beliefs, or even more obscure forms of bonding around symbols (or perhaps more properly memes), these tribes do not restrict themselves to one location or to more traditional kinship forms. They are free-floating schools that coalesce at different times and places, stay in touch through the Internet and continually morph. An architect is someone one can spot almost anywhere in the world, just as one can a Mormon, a punk, or a Prada junkie.

Droog is also a kind of tribe, in which the members, as mentioned above, gain an often temporary (if recurring) identity through the adoption of their designs or their participation in projects around the world. More important than this self-definition, however, is that the images, objects and spaces Droog produces have the effect of acting as stagesets or ritual accoutrements that can engender new kinds of tribes. This is certainly true of such participatory projects as 'do create', but it is also the case with projects that highlight certain rituals in the activities of everyday life. Thus Hella Jongerius' or Gijs Bakker's clever deformation and recladding of tableware, or Peter van der Jagt's doorbell turn the social activity of dining or announcing one's arrival in a home into a dramatic action in which one becomes conscious of playing a role. This is a theme that is especially strong in the work of Richard Hutten, whose strangely shaped furniture encourages chance encounters. Arnout Visser's and Erik Jan Kwakkel's tile system turns especially those actions that involve the body (bathing, eating, elimination) into parts of a stark white world in which one's actions become even more highlighted and one person's use of a roll of toilet paper is related to another's use of a soap dish in the same grid.

Irony and wit, which after all show that one is 'in the know,' and thus part of a tribe, are a central part of the work. In using a Droog design, one not only shows that one knows what plate to use or how to hold a fork, but that one knows that one is acting at holding the fork. One participates in the guessing game of what an object should or could be used for, what they are made out of, and what their point really is. In Next Architects' garden fence that turns into a ping-pong table, the role playing is made completely explicit.

There is thus a general set of rules that one can derive from an analysis of Droog's work thus far. They mess with production and consumption, they make sustainability into the rhetorical or perhaps even ideological core of their imagery, and they produce implements we can use to stage our own world, doing what we finally could and should expect from design beyond revealing real power (codes) and acting responsibly, which is to help us define ourselves in relationship to others and our world.

If this would seem like a general strategy, it is, and Droog itself has been careful, especially in their most recent publications, to make it clear that they see what they do as part of a larger set of experiments in design. Thus architects such as Decosterd & Rahm in Switzerland or designers such as Constantin Boym in New York are 'doing Droog,' without their work being or even looking like part of the Droog collection. One can even imagine that at some point Droog Design as such will cease to exist, while the tactics developed under that name will continue to develop in unpre-dictable ways.

Yet one should remember that Droog is also a phenomenon that is rooted in place and time. Its Dutchness and its position in reaction to certain developments in Postmodernism have, as noted above, been explicated elsewhere, but it may be worth-while to also generalize on their spatio-temporal position. Thus one could say that Droog is essentially Postmodern in its attitude and methodology. If modernization continually produces new objects, images and landscapes because the very notion of production through technology under the regime of abstract value justifies its notion of progress, then Postmodernism is the critical reflection on, but in, that process. Completely aware of the artifice of our reality, which produces a fundamentally unstable situation controlled by a technology largely out of our individual control, they produce images, objects and spaces that reflect on that condition.

There is a particularly Dutch way of acting in this manner, which is to engage in a sparing preservation of an artificial landscape that has been made at great cost in order to produce a palimpsest in which one can mirror, map and then elide or deform that reality. This is a perhaps complicated way of saying that Droog does, as I have argued previously, respond in a deep and consistent manner to the Dutch condition in which most of the country's core, an artificial land won from the sea and the rivers, has become a three-dimensional puzzle of hybrid forms that are continually rearran-ged to allow for ever more efficient use of space. It is a country in which space and land are continually reused and deformed according to new conditions because they have to be: there is no place else to go except to annex more land from the sea. Moreover, with land being this precious, what is made are not products, but transactions. The Dutch are a trading nation, who operate the codes of commerce (as well of genetic manipulation, in their flower production) with great skill. Their culture thus values both the preservation of existing conditions as well as experimentation that will allow more profitable uses of that reality. They reflect and map this process obsessively, producing an art that displays its own process and disappears into the recombination of what already exists.

Thus Droog are part of a larger Postmodern perspective, of which there are many practitioners, and part of a Dutch perspective, which they share, for instance, with some famous and influential architects and fashion designers. It is that place from which they come that gives them a voice in the global debate on what we should make in our culture, and how and why.

What I love about their particular contribution is its gleefull, unabashed self-consciousness. I also love the things they make. I would argue for Droog as an exultation of the craft of recombination, recoding, reuse and ritual, performed as self-conscious and often quite funny acts. It is what the hippies that were my first role models did forty years ago, and it is what this latter-day band of fun-loving rebels do today. They don't, however, just tune in and drop out, nor do they run around naked on farms. Rather, they are part of a network jetting around the world and influencing designers at every stop. Over the last decade they have in this manner designed a space for themselves as a tribe of homo ludens, building not a utopia, but a New Babylon brick by recycled brick, attracting designers from ever farther afield while threatening continually to dissolve into a myriad voices. Theirs is an edifice that will never be finished, but in ten years they have managed to come quite far in constructing the ironic, self-justifying edifice that is Droog.

use it again

What about a second life for products that are old, worn out, not fashionable anymore or for other reasons do not fit anymore in their environment?

1

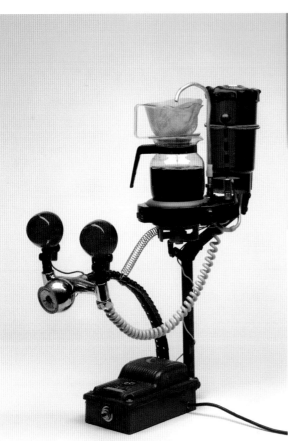

Rag chair

Tejo Remy
1991
rags, steel strips
60 x 60 x 110 cm

Speaking coffee maker

Eibert Draisma
1990
rejected material
variable size

This coffeemaker is assembled
from reject material, including
the base of an old transformer
containing a sample so that
the appliance really can tell you
when the coffee is ready.

use it again

Gareth Williams

Curator of the Architecture Gallery and specialist in contemporary design at the Victoria and Albert Museum, London

Do we realise how wasteful we are? We make too many poorly designed objects that rapidly lose their appeal, or cease to function, or are rendered obsolete. We live in a culture where waste is acceptable, even desirable, and where objects are discarded simply when they no longer seem new. Designers, as the prime authors of objects of desire, have a responsibility to react to this state of affairs, though in truth it is consumers who can really effect change.

In the early 1990s a new morality was observable in design. It was no longer sufficient to design attractive or efficient products. The materials and manufacturing processes also had to be as sustainable and as environmentally friendly as possible. Moreover designers felt it necessary to make overt statements about the environmental credibility of their objects. In Germany design studio Bär and Knell made chairs from waste consumer products that were as much manifestos of political correctness as they were usable items. British designer Jane Atfield made simple furniture from brightly coloured board manufactured from old plastic bottles. The material did not disguise the fact that it was recycled. Numerous designers, inspired by Achille Castiglioni as well as by their consciences, rediscovered the idea of the 'readymade'. Michael Marriot, for example, celebrated the over-looked everyday beauty of sardine tins and hardware store commodities like wing nuts and angle brackets. Recycling was, for a few years around 1994, as much a fashion stance as it was a genuine and deeply held ethic.

As already suggested, designers approach recycling in numerous ways and for different reasons. One proposition is to re-use materials or waste, or objects that are obsolete. This is an attempt to make better use of resources expressed through the recycling of materials. Perhaps more interesting, and intertwined with this approach, is the notion of reusing ideas, memories and archetypes to give objects a sense of longevity: recycling conceptual values. Both approaches are present in Tejo Remy's chest of drawers, comprised of an assortment of found drawers from discarded old

Jurgen Bey
1999
two way mirror foil,
existing lamp
Ø 39 x 81 cm

The two-way mirror
lightshade conceals
an old, worn out
or unfashionable lamp.
At daytime the
mirroifoil reflects its
environment.
Turned on, the hidden
lamp appears in
new clothes.

furniture, each encased in new timber carcases. The impression of deliberate yet casual salvage is heightened because the drawers are slung together at precarious angles. Remy called the object 'You canít lay down your memories' and spoke of the individual character and memories encapsulated in each different drawer.

Reusing components from other artefacts is not a new method. Achille Castiglioni famously re-used a metal tractor seat for his Mezzadro stool in 1957. His Toio lamp of 1962 is an assemblage of car parts and bare electrical components. These appear to have integrity as designed objects because of their honest approach to appropriation. It is as if the designer is acknowledging that the forms he has borrowed cannot be improved upon. In the 1980s Ron Arad and the Creative Salvage team also appropriated their materials, but for them the source was not the factory but the scrap heap. The recycled results, such as Arad's Rover Chair, spoke of nothing less than post-industrial decay and post-apocalyptic doom. They were also extravagant style statements that set out to shock us into re-examining design conventions. Similarly, Eibert Draisma's Speaking Coffee Maker tells us that electrical products do not have to be slick or high-tech to function and viewed as such it is a bedfellow of Arad's iconic concrete stereo.

Chest of drawers

Tejo Remy
1991
used drawers, maple
60 x 110 x 120 cm

Jurgen Bey's salvage of discarded and obsolete objects is less casual than Remy's and more pastoral. He recognises worth and value in an unfashionable or damaged object that can be revived, heightened and given a new lease of life. Metaphorically and literally he re-skins and bandages up objects to heal their wounds and make them last another day. They are elegiac essays on the potential of objects to evoke our memories. He educates us to find beauty in imperfection. Ideas expounded by the Netherlands Design Institute in the 1990s and books like Eternally Yours (1996) pointed the way to a re-evaluation of objects focusing primarily on a product's longevity. Longevity achieved through emotional or symbolic appeal is aside from the reuse of materials and recycling per se. Imbuing objects with expressive values so we want to keep them for longer is a mechanism for short-circuiting rapid obsolescence. It is this approach that we see most clearly in the objects illustrated here. The archetypal qualities of some of these objects (the bourgeois lamps in Jurgen Bey's Light Shade Shade, for example) are exploited because of their nostalgic resonance. They remind us of core values: that there is validity in memory and the past; that 'new' is not automatically better than 'old'; that content and purpose are as important as style and appearance.

Similar ideas lie behind Gijs Bakker's Peepshow wallpaper that features a cut design allowing spots of the old paper underneath to show through. It regulates and heightens our perception of an older product. Rather then sublimating or replacing the past, history and memory are used again as core conceptual elements of the new design.

Nostalgia plays a part in the way these designers have reused the past. Max Wolf, Markus Bader and Sebastian Oschatz are younger than Bakker or Bey and the past they revisit in their Bootleg objects is relatively recent but no less nostalgic. The collection comprises obsolete hi-fi equipment fitted with up-to-date MP3 technology serving the same function. It is a curious marriage of the past and present in which both are compromised. The project fails to be a commentary on built-in obsolescence as one technology has utterly superseded the other. Perhaps the designers sought to celebrate the aesthetic of Dieter Rams 1962 'Cinderella's coffin' record player or a Technics deck from 1980, both of which have their place in design history. But neither the iconic older products nor the new technology are improved by their collision. The project is more open-ended and less resolved than the others discussed here.

Design fashions pass and it is too soon to know whether reuse as a design concept will stand the test of time. Will the ideas explored here appear as superannuated as the Hi-fi equipment revived in the Bootleg objects? We know we must become more sustainable in the ways we produce, consume and dispose of our products. For the time being, designs like these are testaments to our need to change our ways. Yet they can only be ciphers or symbols of what is possible through design.

Vase 'Monte Azul'

Nadine Sterk, Lonny van Rijkwijck
2005
wood, plastic bottles
Ø 19 x 20 cm

Plastic containers for household cleaning products are given a second life by using them as a sealed interior for a wooden vase. The vases are being produced in a woodworking shop in the Monte Azul favela in Sao Paolo, Brazil. The vases originated in a project by the Design Academy Eindhoven aimed at stimulating international distribution for this workshop through design. In December 2004, Droog organised an auction of ten 'do scratch' lamps by designer Martí Guixé on which ten cartoonists and artists scratched their drawings. The revenue from the auction was invested in woodworking equipment for the Monte Azul manufacturing firm so that they can handle bigger quantities.

Jan Konings,
Jurgen Bey
1997/99
PVC coating,
existing furniture
variable size

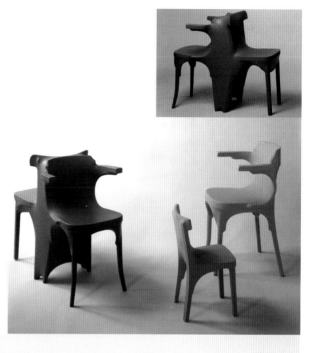

Doormat 'Hommage to Gerd Arntz'

Ed Annink
1993
black and brown coco mat
various sizes

Many old pictograms by Gerd Arntz were available to be used for statistics. Through the interference of Ed Annink they became doormats.

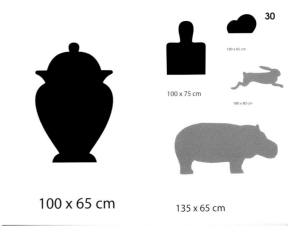

100 x 65 cm

180 x 80 cm

100 x 75 cm

100 x 65 cm

135 x 65 cm

What are we to learn from the frugality and prudence of recycled design objects? They are exercises in 'making do and mending' and as such they are indictments of our wasteful ways. They are not luxurious, but neither are they particularly functional. Perhaps it is their modesty and the humility of their execution that is their greatest lesson. They are polemical objects that dare us to keep consuming wastefully.

do reincarnate

Martí Guixé
2000
Nylon thread, fitting, existing lamp
Ø 10 x 30 cm

Revive your old lamp by using
it in a different way. Just hang it.

St. Petersburg chair

Jurgen Bey
2003
existing chair, foam,
glass reinforced Polyester
46 x 52 x 104 cm
Picture: Dutch Room St. Petersburg

This chair was developed for
the Dutch Room in St.Petersburg.
It is an antique chair covered
with layers of fiberglass. The final
layer has been silk-screened
with a flower pattern.

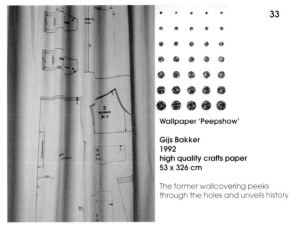

Wallpaper 'Peepshow'

Gijs Bakker
1992
high quality crafts paper
53 x 326 cm

The former wallcovering peeks
through the holes and unveils history

Curtain with
dressmaker's pattern

Djoke de Jong
1993
print on cotton
various sizes

When you decide to change
the curtain, you can use
the printed image as a pattern
for a jacket.

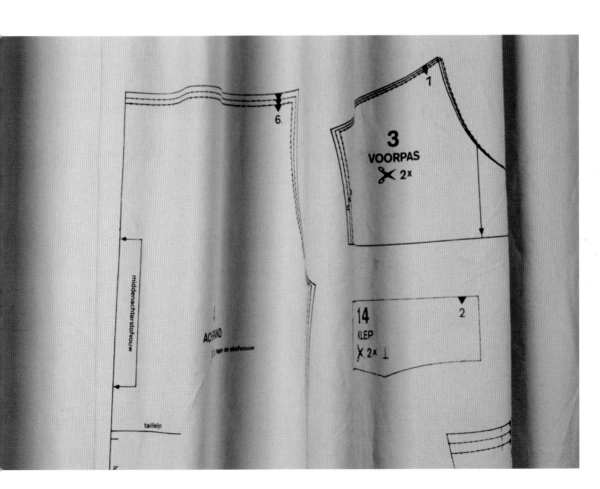

**Max Wolf, Markus Bader,
Sebastian Oschatz
2003**

Latest Technology (MP3
Jukebox/Server and custom
developed Interfaces)
inserted into vintage icons
of HiFi history - the Technics
SP1210 from 1980, a Bang
& Olufsen system from 1973,
and Dieter Rams' 1962
Braun Audio 1. Built to order
upon request.

Watch 'Time Pieces'

**Itay Noy
2005
used watches and various materials
various sizes**

In his project 'Time Pieces', Itay Noy analyses the filter
of time in two respects: the material and the look.
The photo of an old broken-down watch indicates
the time the watch stopped running. This photo is
put into the old case with a new mechanism and
new glass. An inner dialogue is created between the
old image and the new one.

familiar - not so familiar

We all know that familiar things are important in our lives. But we also know that we do want new things too. A logical solution would be to combine the two. The familiar applied in a new way.

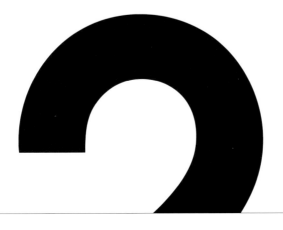

familiar - not so familiar

Louise Schouwenburg

Artist and writer

Many of the products in the Droog Design collection play an intriguing game with memory. The work of Jurgen Bey, for example, can easily be associated with the elegant chairs and large winged armchairs from a time long ago when furniture lasted for generations. Or the way that Marcel Wanders, Gijs Bakker, Dick van Hoff and others often use forms and decorative patterns that are universally known and could even be called archetypal. We know immediately what we are seeing, we recognise them and only notice a certain strangeness on second glance.

'Why should I invent new forms if reality already offers so many fantastic images, so many special solutions. As a designer I only have to discover them and to restructure them into new stories', says Bey.

As Marcel Proust described in his wonderful search for times past (A la recherche du temps perdu, 1913), old pieces of furniture have stories and memories are attached to them. Proust found this mainly in what he calls trivial, everyday objects such as 'the lamp of Bohemian glass, shaped like an urn and hung by chains from the ceiling'.

This lamp was worth cherishing; after all, it provided access to precious feelings that were in danger of disappearing into the distant mists of memory.

This is similar to what Bey means when he talks about images that are already to be found in reality. But there's more to it than that in his work. 'The suspicion that there are stories hidden under the skin of objects is immensely fascinating.' However logical this may sound, it is by no means self-evident that the significance of objects not only transcends their functionality but also their capacity to absorb our personal memories. Even before the user can link his own experiences to Bey's chairs they already mean something, they are already telling an intriguing story. Bey has given them a voice.

According to the German philosopher Heidegger, the role played by use-objects is quite limited. They are mainly meant to be instrumental and reliable. In contrast to

Knotted chair

Marcel Wanders
1996
carbon and aramid fibers, epoxy
50 x 60 x 100 cm

The rope made of an aramid braid
is knotted into the shape of
a chair. Then the slack texture is
impregnated with epoxy
and hung in a frame to harden.

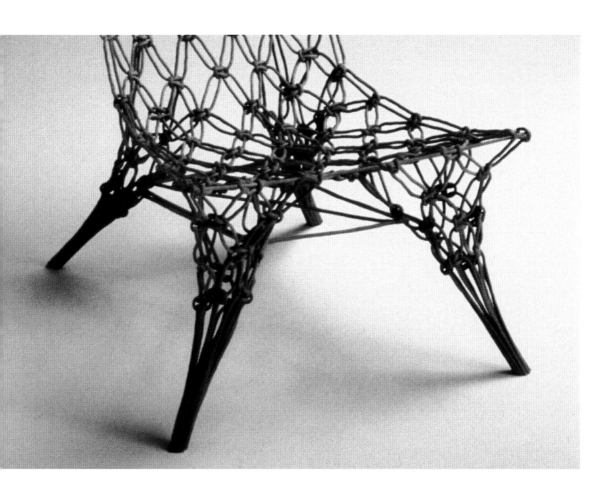

works of art, use-objects are slowly but surely consumed in being used, since the objects coincide with their function. With works of art it is very different. They do not use themselves up, their presence is what counts. Of course such a definition of use-objects from 1935 is quite dated. yet it does help us gain more insight into the effect of conceptual design. If Heidegger is to be believed then use-objects have a tragic fate; if they function well we don't even notice them any more. You feel a shoe as soon as it pinches, but if it fits well then it disappears, as it were, from your consciousness. That does not seem in keeping with contemporary use-objects which usually shout loudly for attention, They seize upon all possible means, including aggressive use of colour, intense design and a profusion of technical possibilities. Helped by all these tricks they above all demand the attention of the consumer; there are, after all, a lot of interests at stake. But this attention generally doesn't last very long. Utterly charmed, we cherish our new mobile phone for a few hours after purchasing it. After that it simply has to work well and as soon as it needs replacing then we chuck away the old one with the greatest of ease. Otherwise, to paraphrase Heidegger, it would start to attract attention because of its irritating shortcomings and we don't want to grant it such attention. So cherishing it was not such a big deal after all. The desire for the latest gadget is perhaps more important than the possession. In the case of electronics we can still talk about an inherent time factor, but a similar contact is noticeable with objects like furniture or clothes. 'Buying is illusion, owning is disillusion', as Dutch writer Bas Heijne has written in one of his essays (2002). Apparently what we desire is something different than what things can give.

Works of art are not so quickly ready for the garbage. We don't buy a painted panel but an illusory story, not an object but ideas, not a thing but implicit beauty, and these we don't throw away so quickly. That use-objects also possess a value that transcends their thingness was convincingly illustrated by Proust. Trivial use-objects can awaken memories, but there's more to it than that. Functional objects can also tell a story of their own, as with Meret Oppenheim's fur-covered cup and saucer from 1936. A more recent art installation also shows the narrative power of use-objects: Dutch artist Zeger Reyers piled up a huge mountain of crockery on a 15 metre long covered table ('Good Intentions', 1997). Both Oppenheim and Reyers make an intervention that allows use-objects to tell an intriguing story about conventions, etiquette and the growth of consumption and excess. But it is indeed at the expense of functionality.

Functionality does not necessarily have to be lost in order to guarantee artistic value, as Jurgen Bey shows in virtually all his work. By sliding a semi-transparent plastic shade over an old chandelier, for example, an old lamp is suddenly made to say something new. As soon the light is turned on the chandelier becomes visible. The modern lamp is only given its due once the past is illuminated and if the object doesn't function we just see opaque modern design without roots: a closed universe. The deeper layers of

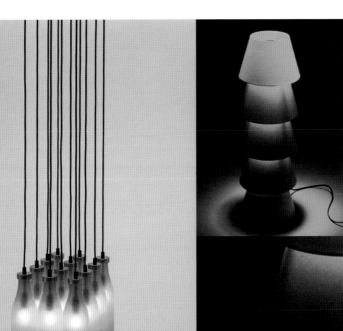

Lamp 'Set up shades'

Marcel Wanders
1988
existing lampshades
Ø 15 x 55 cm

Milkbottle lamp

Tejo Remy
1991
milk bottles , 15 W bulbs
36 x 27 x 310 cm

Three times a row of four
bottles, exactly as it is
in a Dutch milk crate.

Treetrunk bench

Jurgen Bey
1999
bronze casts of existing chairs, treetrunk
400 x 70 x 85 cm

meaning are not immediately noticeable perhaps, the lamp simply functions well, but it slowly dawns on one that it works on all levels and is not merely an old product with a modern veneer. Designers like Bey play with the associations and histories surrounding lamps, chairs and crockery, bringing these associations to the fore, as it were. The result is an intriguing tension between function and meaning. To use Heidegger's terminology, they wear themselves out as use-objects, while as art objects they emphasize an unmistakable autonomous quality.

Two other good examples are Marcel Wanders' 'Knotted Chair' and Gijs Bakker's 'Knitted Maria'. The chair by Wanders reveals its story immediately: I am made of knotted rope yet strong enough to serve as a chair. Despite the immediacy the object remains intriguing. The built-in tension between expectation and immediacy is not solved within the image of the chair. We may well suspect ingenious high tech but that doesn't make any difference. Wanders has not just opened a cheap box of tricks, the rope will say each time anew that it cannot possibly be a chair. Bakker also thwarts expectations. The knitting around the archetypal coffee pot tells a story that perhaps the pot itself no longer tells because we have seen it so often. We see a world of domestic comfort appearing before our mind's eye, we see generations sitting at the table, pottering around in the house, intimacy and oppressive coziness. Maybe we even see a coffee pot fallen to pieces and held together by neat knitting. The imagination is challenged.

Not only people and works of art, but also the everyday things we surround ourselves with, are sometimes not what they seem. What makes conceptual use-objects so interesting is the tension between a certain disappearing into over familiar and reliable functionality while at the same time they make themselves subtly known by telling something about themselves. Unlike easily disposable gadgets, they appeal not so much to the urge to purchase but mainly cause a different way of seeing. There's a great deal to discover behind the flimsy skin of everyday things.

Vase 'Urn'

Hella Jongerius
1993
soft PU
Ø 21 x 23 cm

This soft vase is based on
a familiar shape. The vase
hides nothing, the traces
of its making are still there.
It is a mass of scratches
and bubbles, the edge is
frayed, even the moulding
joints are visible. There is
nothing to tell us how old
this product is.

Birdhouse

Marcel Wanders
2000
recycled plastic, porcelain plate
20 x 30 x 20 cm

Straps

NL Architects
2000
silicon rubber
70 x 3 x 1 cm

Sugar cage

Sophie Lachaert, Luc d'Hanis
2005
silver
14 x 9,5 x 10 cm

Bas Warmoeskerken
2005
polystyrene
various sizes

A mediaeval tea service
from the Dutch town of
Bergen op Zoom is made
with contemporary materials
and in accordance with
today's production methods,
including all the imperfections
that are visible in the
original service.

Wieki Somers
& Dylan van den Berg
2001
okoume plywood
70 x 30 x 201 cm

Digital cuckoo clock 'nest'

Cynthia Hathaway
2002
digital display, cuckoo clock
mechanism, bird's nest
25 x 150 x 25 cm

Jurgen Bey, Sophie Krier,
Ed van Driel
2004
acrylic
158 x 67 x 90 cm /
100 x 67 x 90 cm

A new version of the old tea
table using the technique of
blister packaging. Originally
designed for the Simply Droog
exhibition.

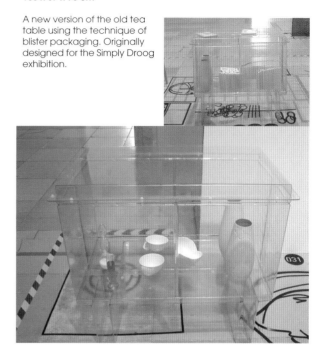

Wall clock 'Time Pieces'

Itay Noy
2005
photographic paper, wood,
quartz movement
112 x 5 x 142 cm

Different antique wall clocks have been
photographed and scaled to life size. A new
clockwork connected with new hands
make the mechanism work behind the photo.
The sounds of Big Ben have been transferred
into an electronic movement that mimics
exactly the same chords. We can experience
the image we are familiar with, although it is
only two-dimensional. The new clock functions
like the original clock did, but perhaps the only
real comparison is the memory it evokes.

Coffeepot 'Knitted Maria'

Gijs Bakker
1997
porcelain, glaze
Ø 11 x 23 cm

A cosy has been knitted round
the Maria coffeepot, a classic
item in the Rosenthal collection.
The knitted part integrated
with the porcelain during the
glazing process.

Teapot 'High-tech accent'

Gijs Bakker
1997
porcelain, alumina-boria-
silica fibres
Ø 17 x 13 cm

Tile kitchen

Arnout Visser, Erik Jan Kwakkel,
Peter van der Jagt
2001
ceramic, various materials
403 x 198 x 165 cm

open design

If we think about a closer relationship between people and products, we could also think of the user's interference in the design. Letting people interact and play, making products more personal.

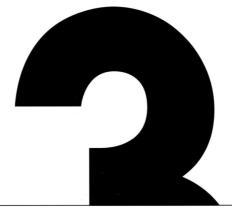

Signature vases

Frank Tjepkema
2003
nylon, stereo lithography
various sizes approx. 30 x 20 x 15 cm

open design

Jaakko van 't Spijker

Architect and founding partner in studio
Sputnik, office for architecture, urbanism
and research, in Rotterdam

Everyone is an original! That is the premise of a lot of advertising, television shows, travel organisations, mobile phone providers, designer fashion labels, furniture chains, etc[1]. The more frequent this kind of rhetoric is exerted, the more poignant its message becomes: individual identity is in deep trouble and desperately needs regular recharging. Not to worry, however; buy this or that product, and your unique you will be all right for some time. Individuality is being mass produced and sold, and this is where the trouble kicks in. There is an almost mathematical correlation between the rise of mass production and the erosion of unicity and individuality. This paradox is faced by every design discipline, from the large scale of the city and buildings in urbanism and architecture, to the scale of the object in fashion and industrial product design. Thus, ironically, most design products are trapped in a vicious circle. The more successful they are, the less they are able to meet the demands of unicity[2].

Experientialising is the keyword for making things feel unique. In the course of the last two decades experience has become the engine of consumer society[3]. Within the new experience economy two design attitudes have developed, that address experience in a totally opposing manner: closed and open specificity (open = undefined; specific = highly defined). Out of these two positions, the first pretends to deliver unique experiences, whereas the second actually does provoke unpredictable and thus per definition one-of-a-kind reactions. Compare for instance any kid's furniture from Lundia or IKEA with Djoke de Jong's Drawing Table and Maartje Steenkamp's Children's Chair. It is immediately clear how essentially different the latter two are. They are and they are not a means to an end. Brand new, they are finished and simultaneously haven't even started their lives yet.

Closed specificity is employed to please people, as often with the best intentions as simply to make money. This kind of attitude is attractive for both hard-core idealists

Drawing table

Djoke de Jong
1993
MDF, schoolboard paint
100 x 65 x 78 cm

Pallet

Martijn Hoogendijk
1993
beech
170 x 68 x 12 cm

This product has as many
purposes as you can
discover in it yourself.

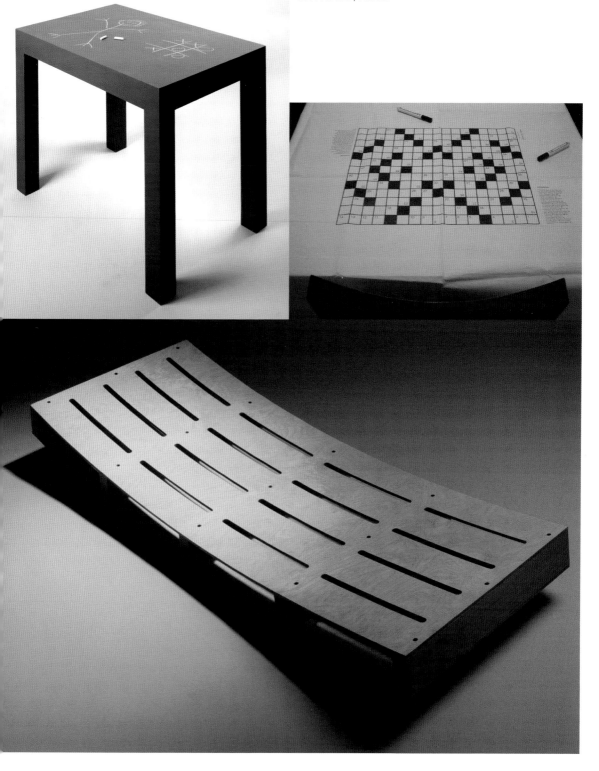

do scratch

Martí Guixé
2000
lighting armature, black coating
27 x 27 x 5 cm

The black surface has to be scratched
with a personal choice of graffiti before
it becomes a lamp.

Marijn van der Pol
2000
1.25 mm stainless
steel, hammer
100 x 70 x 75 cm

A hammer is supplied
to finish the design
of this chair. Hit and
sculpt the shape
you want it to be.

do break

Frank Tjepkema,
Peter van der Jagt
2000
porcelain, rubber, silicon
Ø 15 x 34 cm

The porcelain vase is covered
inside with a layer of silicon
rubber. After you have bought
it you can smash it. The silicon
holds the shards in place, and
the owner then has a unique vase.

do add 'short leg'

Jurgen Bey
2000
laminate, chromium
plated steel, rubber
40 x 45 x 83 cm

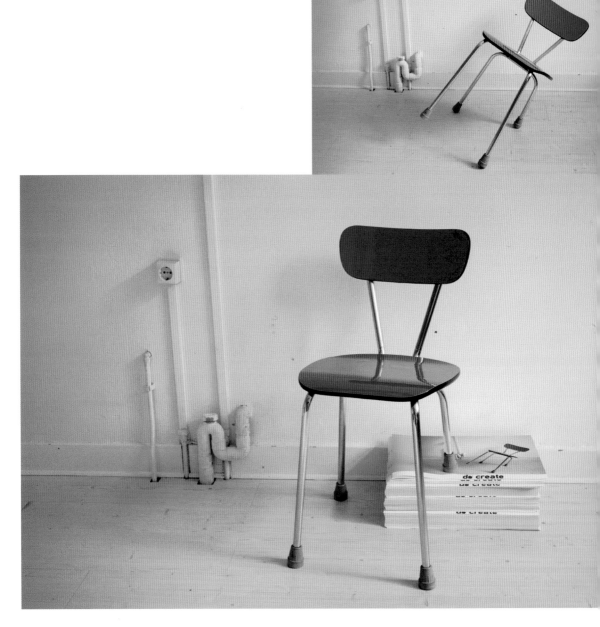

do frame

Martí Guixé
2000
self adhesive vinyl tape
5 cm, 25 meter roll

Arrange strips of the ornately printed tape to create your own golden frame around any surface you desire.

(New-Age merchandising) and hard-core capitalists (Disney merchandising). Whatever the motive behind it, closed specific products don't allow much space for interpretation. That is why it is also possible to talk about 'dead-end specificity'.

Open specificity lacks any ambition whatsoever to embody good intentions in an ideological sense. It may shock (Benetton adverts), it may tease (Richard Hutten's The Cross and Table-Stool; Tejo Remy's Chest of Drawers) but it certainly does not appease. You might say that besides being outspoken and extravagant this approach is also pragmatic and even indifferent. Open specificity is interested exclusively in its own agenda, and by doing so leaves space for anyone's own interpretation. This level of freedom defines its attractiveness[4].

The distinction between open and closed forms of specificity is the degree to which the perception of these is prescribed or predetermined. In other words, in a case of open specificity the experience that the concept might trigger is not hinted at, even though it is indeed present. Consider Hector Serrano's Clothes Hanger lamp. Once the owner actually uses it, they transform their daily outfit to light the room. The Clothes Hanger lamp simultaneously disappears and comes to life. The impact of something that is open specific does not become clear until it reaches the receiving end: the user/viewer. The open and closed approaches are also often tellingly expressed in com-mercials. There are adverts which establish an atmosphere and say very little about the product (mobile telephones, cigarettes): they are specific yet open. In contrast to this, consider washing powder adverts: a washing powder ad is 80 percent solid information, data that is embellished with a meagre 20 percent atmosphere: they are specific but closed.

Droog Design clearly likes the open side of this spectrum. They have stretched the open specific attitude beyond physical products to mere image: A wonderful example of this kind of thinking is do, the brand developed by advertising agency KesselsKramer. The most important notion behind do is that it is a brand name which runs ahead of the product. First there was the brand, and then whoever wanted to furnish a product that fitted the brand was welcome to do so. The do mission statement states: 'do is an ever-changing brand that depends on what you do. Somewhere in the future is a brand that you are creating. It is a brand that responds to your ideas, feelings, and thinking. It is a brand that is flexible enough to allow lots of people to be involved. This wacky, future brand is a way to make new and different products and services for people who like to think and do.'[5]

This might all sound terribly abstract, but various products which put the philosophy simply and clearly into practice have been developed under the do flag. The common denominator for this series of remarkable projects is their ability to combine mass

Rag chair
with scottish rags

Tejo Remy
1991
rags, steel strips
60 x 60 x 110 cm

Chest of drawers

**Tejo Remy
1991
used drawers, maple
60 x 110 x 120 cm**

The chest has no fixed form.
You can strap the drawers
together like you wish. You
can exchange drawers or
you can add other personal
belongings, like a wine rack
or a tv set.

production and individual identity. Do, and for that matter a whole range of Droog
Design products, have added a new dimension to the word customisation. The 'do
break', for example, is a porcelain vase covered inside with a layer of latex. After you
have bought it you can smash it. The latex holds the shards in place, and the owner
then has a unique vase. The 'do hit' is an aluminium cube that the purchaser can
bash with a mallet, transforming it into a personal seat. And the list goes on. The do
brand specializes in all kinds of disciplines, surprising combinations and products,
all of which share the common feature of reserving an active role for the consumer.

Because an open specific approach offers limited information, this has an unexpected
side effect: In a curious and sometimes even unsettling way it is more authentic than
closed specificity. The latter somehow often parallels conservatism. In the closed
specific branding of shop and restaurant chains for example, we often encounter
references to a kind of good-old-days security blanket: homegrown, old country,
original, arts and crafts. The selection of these kinds of brand names acknowledges
the need for identity and unicity, but the infill is dull and transparent. The allusions
that are made by closed specific products are often hypocritical (mass-produced

Clothes hanger lamp

Hector Serrano
2002
acrylic, fluorescent light 11 W
41 x 22 x 5 cm

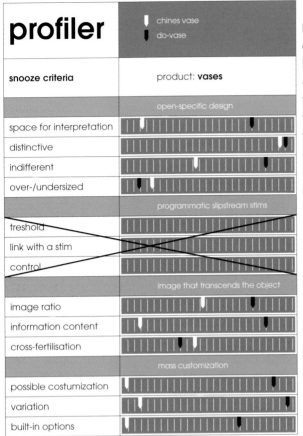

profiler

chines vase
do-vase

snooze criteria	product: **vases**
	open-specific design
space for interpretation	
distinctive	
indifferent	
over-/undersized	
	programmatic slipstream stims
treshold	
link with a stim	
control	
	image that transcends the object
image ratio	
information content	
cross-fertilisation	
	mass customization
possible costumization	
variation	
built-in options	

bread is still mass-produced bread, even if it does have a 'homegrown' label) but they work. The open approach is less literal. This means that it is less prone to hypocritical forms of fake. There is as little need for message or product to be true as with closed specificity, but at least no pretension of truth is presented (Tejo Remy's Milk Bottle lamp and Gijs Bakker's Wallpaper 'Peepshow' illustrate this). The warped authenticity of open specificity totally relies on the space afforded for interpretation.

It is fascinating that an approach which can permit itself to be wayward, ambiguous and even in a certain sense authentic has evolved in the world of design. It is an intelligent response to glamorous adverts, it is an alternative for pretentious and empty company images and in the world of design the consumer becomes involved with the product. Droog Design has intuitively registered this potential gap in the market in developing a range of open specific products. The riddle of open specific design is a fascinating and wayward answer to the paradox of identity in a world of mass production. For people who like to think and DO!

This text is an adapted version of the chapter 'Specificity, open and closed' from the book SNOOZE, immersing architecture in mass culture by studio Sputnik.

Wallpaper
'Peepshow'

Gijs Bakker
1992
high quality crafts
paper
53 x 326 cm

Children's highchair

Maartje Steenkamp
2003
wood, saw, sandpaper
40 x 40 x 145 cm

. 'Everyone is an original' was the 2001 slogan in an advertising campaign for Chesterfield cigarettes.

his is just one of the countless examples of advertising aimed at the unique identity of potential consumers

e. Nokia ('unleash your creativity/a sign of attitude'), Wallpaper ('the stuff that surrounds you'), etc. etc.

. 'Identity is like a mousetrap in which more and more mice have to share the original bait.' Rem Koolhaas,

he Generic City, SMLXL, 1995, page 1248.

. In their book The ExperienceEconomy the economists Gimore and Pine argue that no form of economic

ctivity generates as much added value as the staging of experiences. This 'experience' is essentially different

o service or comfort. It is a new category of added value. James H. Gilmore & B.J. Pinell, The Experience

conomy, work is theatre & every business a stage, Boston, 1999.

. The concept 'open specificity' is related to the openness of artworks as discussed by Umberto Eco in

he Open Work. In this book, Eco describes how certain artworks expect an interpretation from the 'consumer'

order to be seen to full advantage. Umberto Eco, The Open Work, trans. Anna Cancogni, rev. ed., 1989.

. Extracted from website: www.dosurf.com

Bag collector

Bless
2001
leather, metal clip
30 x 25 x 6 cm

Chest box

Jan Konings
2001
birch plywood
60 x 60 x 40 cm

Red blue chair

Mario Minale
2004
Lego bricks
60 x 60 x 90 cm

inevitable ornament

Droog products are known because of their simplicity. Yet there is decoration. This decoration is part of the concept, follows from the con- cept in a logical, natural way. In some instance the decoration just shows how the product is made and is therefore not identified instantly as decoration.

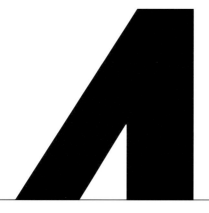

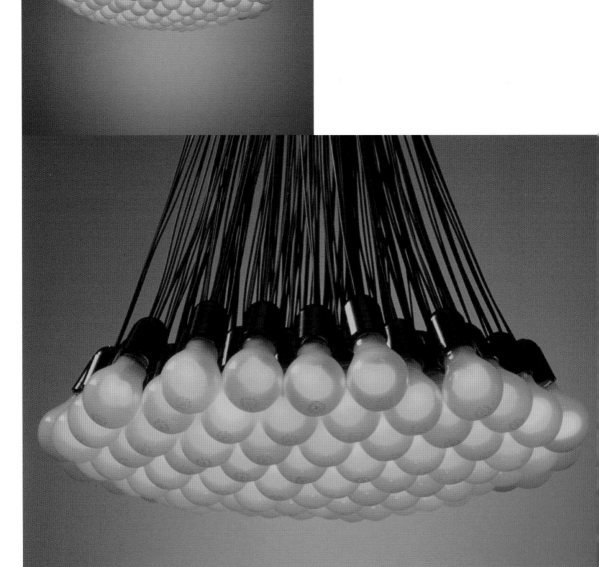

Rody Graumans
1993
85 bulbs 15 W, standard fitting,
dimmer
Ø 60 x 100 cm

inevitable ornament

Louise Schouwenburg

Artist and writer

Simon Heydens has designed interactive wallpaper on which the decorations can be changed at will. The idea of unrestricted freedom of choice for the customer is pushed over the top with considerable irony. It all has to be figured out technically, but in the prototype it already works fantastically.
By means of a computer-driven programme, garlands of flowers change slowly into toy cars which in their turn fade out and are replaced by new emblems. According to Heydens, experiments with current conducting ink are advancing to such an extent that good solutions can be expected in the near future.

Decorative wallpaper, ornaments on furniture, gold and scrollwork on the frame of a painting, embroidery stitches on bedsheets, they're all making a comeback. The ornament, or parergon (supplement, accessory; from the Greek para+ergon = next to the work), is an added beauty that is not necessary, a decoration. According to the French philosopher Jacques Derrida this supplementary beauty is perhaps more important than we suspect (La vérité en peinture, 1978). Maybe the parergon says more than the ergon, the painting's frame more than the painting itself. Derrida, whose name is inextricably linked with deconstructivism, unravelled and deconstructed certain important historical theories about beauty. One theory that until today has been crucial for the way we talk about art is Immanuel Kant's Critique of Judgement, 1790. Kant distinguished the absolute beauty to be found in nature and art from the incidental beauty such as decoration and the painting's frame. Although, according to Kant, all our judgements about beauty are subjective, we can only make so-called 'pure judgements' about the former type, for our attitude is one of disinterested and therefore free delight. With beauty no interest extorts approval and we may therefore expect that others will agree with us. As regards the latter type, the agreeable, we are only able to make an impure, subjective judgement of taste because delight in the agreeable is coupled with interest, of the senses for instance. Tastes may thus differ as far as decoration goes but not in respect of absolute beauty.

Moving Wallpaper

Simon Heijdens
2002
paper, thermo-chrome ink,
silver, silkscreen
200 x 100 x 230 cm

The wallpaper, printed with thermo
sensitive ink and ink that conducts
electricity, can be changed at will.

This hierarchy in types of beauty belonged very much of course to the belief in absolute values which in the 18th century was not yet subject to doubt. But since, as Derrida says, we have reason to doubt The Truth or God, we may also contest the claims to truth of theory, as well as the pure beauty of works of art and the hierarchical relationship between painting and frame. In the margin, in unintended slips, in the framing and between the lines of texts, there is sometimes more to be discovered than in the work or the text itself. It is possible that the decorations on the wallpaper betray more about the inhabitant than the furniture, the works of art on the wall, the choice of partner or the books on the shelves. You're not likely to come across wallpaper with a motif of wild flowers in the homes of admirers of Gerrit Rietveld and Mondrian, indeed no wallpaper at all, but austerely plastered white walls. You find broken white with light relief patterns on the wallpaper mainly in the homes of nice Catholics, while brightly coloured stripes and a lot of gold can often be seen in the houses of aesthetic snobs and night owls. The fans of Heydens' wallpaper will probably be interested much more in the revolutionary innovation than in the decorative patterns, the appearing and disappearing flowers and cars. What's wrong with ornaments? Why did they count as inessentials to be avoided by the vanguard?

Modernism had done with superfluousness, with decoration. Since the 1920s it was believed that the Bauhaus formula of 'form follows function' required a sober, minimalistic language of forms suited to the industrial age. Nor was this austerity completely abandoned when, at the end of the 20th century, the slogan for many designers

Extrusion plates

Dick van Hoff
1997
white and blue porcelain
Ø 25 x 2 cm

Service 'B - set'

Hella Jongerius
1999
porcelain with imprints
various sizes

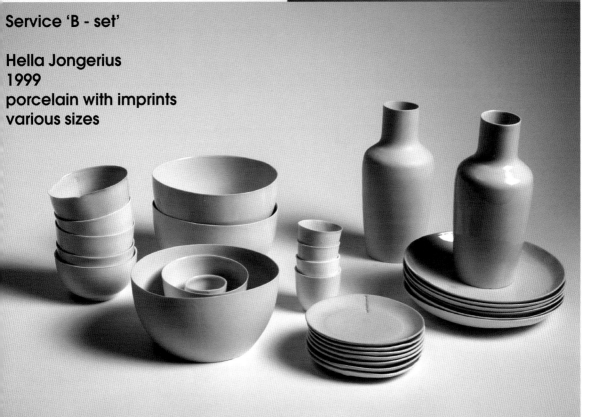

Children's chair 'Bronto'

Richard Hutten
1997
rotation moulded soft and
hard PU
55 x 28 x 35 cm

Cow chair

Niels van Eijk
1997
one cow skin
44 x 38 x 72 cm

changed into 'form follows concept'. Dutch designers working in a conceptual way henceforth allowed themselves more liberties such as humour, stories and meanings that extend beyond the function. But the means they used for this were usually very simple, because they still had to be justified, no longer by function but by concept. Decoration and the traces of craftsmanship and manufacture would indeed reconquer territory in the conceptual quarter, but actually in a different guise than what we are used to with traditional disciplines.

Although painting and sculpture were superseded at the end of the 20th century by less material media, designers were in fact emphasising more and more the physical character of their products. Marcel Wanders, Dick van Hoff, Rody Graumans and Hella Jongerius made the traces of fabrication, deliberate faults in the manufacturing process and accidental residues an essential part of their work. Designers of course are less able than artists to get round the physical character of their work. Their profession is largely devoted to the physical presence of things. Whether they want to or not, they usually have to relate themselves to the skin. So why not emphasise the skin then? This is one way of explaining the reaction from the conceptual quarter. Instead of polishing away all the skin's unevenness, as the industry had been doing for years, thereby equating beauty with smoothness and perfection, the traces of manufacture were now heavily stressed. In Rody Graumans' '85 lamps' the function even merges with the ornament. The bundle of ordinary lightbulbs and the knot of chandelier connections on top are at the same time technical necessities as well as decorative accents. Dick van Hoff's washbasin triumphantly reveals its welding seams and Hella Jongerius' Urn vases show their burrs: the viewer first sees hand-moulded, archetypal urns with thick walls, but a closer study reveals that the urns are thin porcelain casts, delicate copies of their coarse models. Just as the visible seams in the clothes by Martin Margiela and other fashion designers created a new fashion, the aesthetically justified traces of manufacture illustrate a new view not only of design but also of an outdated order of priority between beauty and decoration. Inevitable skin becomes inevitable ornament. According to Jongerius, for whom decoration would become more and more important in her work, it's mainly the small details that stick in our minds. 'We remember the patterns of the wallpaper in the bedroom or the stripes on the coffee cup that we held every day. Forms disappear from memory but decoration lingers.' It seems that conceptual design and decoration are very compatible, as long as the underlying idea gives rise to it. Ornaments can even be inevitable. In Graumans' design as well as in that of Joris Laarman, decoration and function coincide. Laarman graduated in 2003 from the Design Academy with an opulent radiator that seemed to refer more to Rococo decoration than to functional, industrial design. The radiator consists of variable tendrils. It looks postmodern, like a quotation from an old style, but on closer examination it is rather a reinterpretation of modernist form following function. As Laarman found out by studying it, a radiator functions by occupying as large an area as possible. Existing minimalistic radiators, therefore, hardly function optimally, their form seems to be merely a clear artistic interpretation of modernism's formal austerity. In functional terms the requirement of sober design is unsound as the only option for form following function. Laarman's alternative opens perspectives, which is why it is significantly called 'Reinventing Functionality'.

Joris Laarman
2003
concrete, plumbing parts
various sizes

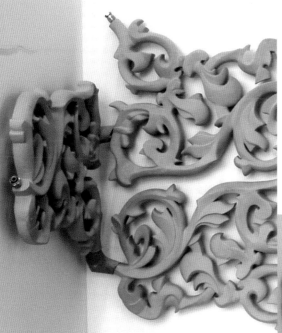

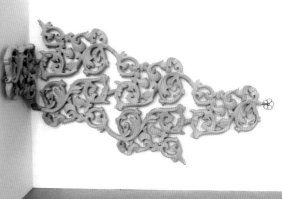

Hot spot pain relief T-shirt

Susanne Philippson
2002
cotton, cherry stones

Once heated in the micro-
wave the cherry stones
will keep your belly warm.

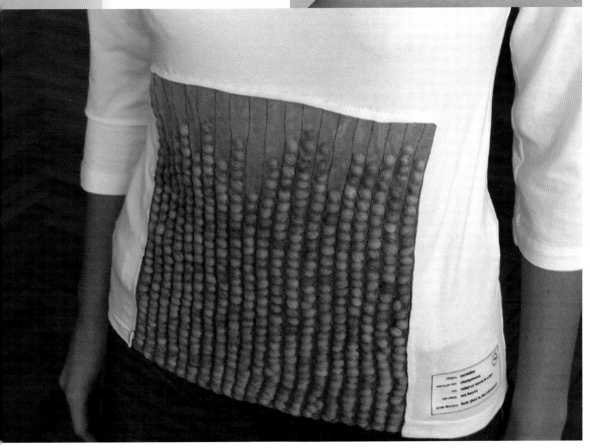

Blooming over cup

Jan B., Mina Wu
2005
Porcelain, transfer print
Ø 5.5 x 9 cm

Porcelain cup designed by Jan B. and decorated with a flower print by Mina Wu. During the Salone del Mobile 2005 in Milan, Droog presented 'Value for Money', a project linking the factors that determine the price of a product to its emotional values. The public was offered different options with corresponding prices and were asked to express their preference. Three different versions of a porcelain cup by Jan B. represented different ways of treatment: one without decoration, one with a transfer print by Mina Wu and one with the same ornament, painted by hand, being the most expensive piece. The transfer print version turned out to be the number one favourite.

Bloom socket

Mina Wu
2004
plastic, ink
10 x 3 x 20 cm

The light switch is so common
that hardly anyone ever
notices it. Mina Wu turned it
into a decorative object by
hand-painted flowers that
grow from the switch over the
wall. Custom-made designs
are possible.

Floral shower T-shirt

by Mina Wu
2005
95 % cotton, 5 % elastan
S, M, L

Whereas the armpit of a T-shirt is not usually
the most attractive part of the shirt, because of
possible sweat stains, Mina Wu turns it into
something positive by making a decorative print
of flowers growing out of it, both on the inside
and on the outside of the shirt.

Table cloth 'Table shapes'

Chris Kabel
2004
100% trevira
280 x 160 x 0.3 cm

Table cloth suitable for
different table shapes. The paper
patterns for the various shapes
form a decorative interplay
of lines. The patterns have been
executed in different kinds of
dotted lines, varying from
small holes to long streaks and
from thin lines to broad stripes.

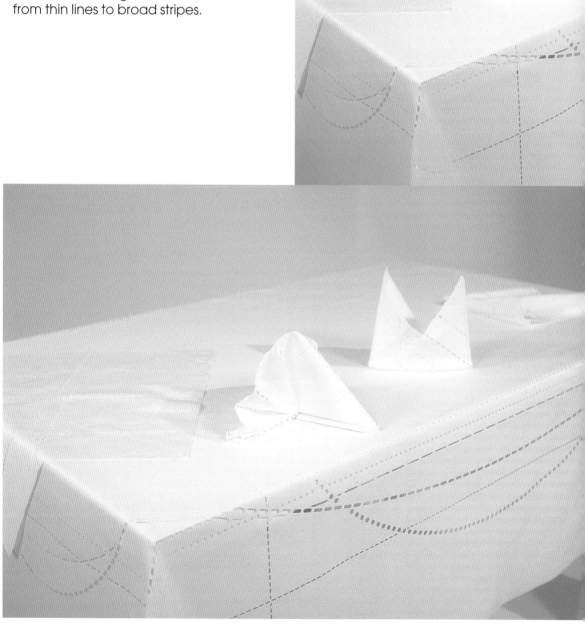

Sugar spoon 'MP' and 'DB'

Ed Annink, Ontwerpwerk
2005
silver
13 x 2.5 cm

Series of two sugar spoons, inspired by
the classic Dutch spoon 'Hollands Glad'.
One of the spoons is titled MP, and was
designed by Ed Annink for the Dutch
Minister President. It was commissioned on
the occasion of the Dutch EU presidency
in 2004 and was offered as a promotional
gift to foreign government leaders.
Whereas in the past sugar spoons were
used to bring sugar from the sugar bowl
to the cup, sugar cubes and sugar bags
have made this use redundant. A hole
has been made in the head of the spoon,
as to emphasise the spoon is solely used
for stirring. A second variation is titled DB.
Starting from the same base form, an open
decoration has been made, inspired on
Delft Blue decoration.

Felt washbasin

Dick van Hoff
1996
felt, polyester
46 x 50 x 40 cm

The idea was to extend
the felt normally used to repair
drain pipes into a wash basin.
The felt parts are sewn together
with black stitching which has
a decorative effect.

Parasol 'Shadylace'

Chris Kabel
2004
wood, steel, PE
Ø 210 x 235 cm

Parasol casting
shadows of branches
and leaves, giving
you the impression of
sitting under a tree
with a bird on top.

Artificial plant

Frank Tjepkema
1996
Plastic, Rubber
50 x 50 x 15 cm

By using the existing ingredients
in a different way, artificial
plants are given an original quality.

Condensation bowls

Arnout Visser
1998
glass, water
Ø 18 x 21 / Ø 24 x 18 cm

In between the inner and outer glasswall there is water and vapour. When the bowl is filled with a hot liquid there is damp, followed by drops on the inside of the glass. When the bowl is then put in the freezer, a pattern of ice flowers is created.
The ornament is not static but develops from a physical process activited by the user.

Arnout Visser
1998
glass
Ø 7 x 11 cm

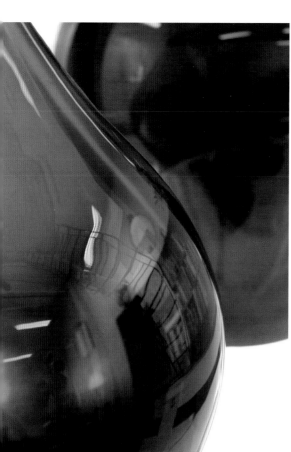

Front
2004
Ø 25 x 40 cm
acrylic

Reflections of surroundings
are inserted in the decoration
of the vase. The reflections
of the new surroundings mix with
the old ones, casting an image
of the history of the vase.

Stakhanov ceramics

Joris Laarman
2005
Ø 11.5 x 6.5 cm
ceramics

Seemingly simple cups form a decorative object as
soon as you stack them up.

simplicity

Droog products are as basic and as minimal as can be: that they consist only of what is needed to materialize the concept. But usually the concept dictates 'more': less and more literally coming together in one product.

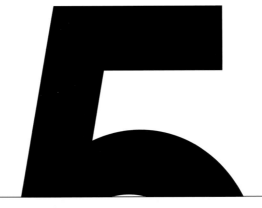

Leon Ramakers, Jan Hoekstra
2005
silicon
Ø 12 x 8 cm

Who is afraid of drilling
into tiled walls? A flexible
hanger that sticks onto
tiled walls, mirrors and
windows by suction, by just
pushing your thumb into
the middle of the object.
The pushed form resembles
a donut. Easy to attach
and remove.

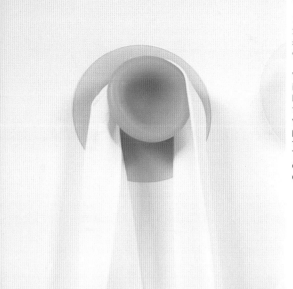

Sugar cubes numbered 1 – 200

Simon Heijdens, United Statements
2003
sugar cubes
chocolate print
17 x 5 x 23 cm

simplicity

Ellen Lupton

Curator of contemporary design at Cooper-Hewitt, National Design Museum in New York and director of the graduate program in graphic design at Maryland Institute College of Art in Baltimore.

For the avant-garde designers of the 1920s and 30s, the quest for simplicity meant cleansing objects of ornament and historical reference. This ritual act of purification was often achieved through the refined, time-consuming finishing of surfaces and materials. Such sublime objects of high modernism as the Barcelona chair were simple in their geometric conception, but not simple to produce. Nor were they simple to live with, as they pleaded for isolation in an austere environment devoid of kitsch, memorabilia, and the passing fancies of habitation. In the1960s and 70s young designers rejected such ponderous views of simplicity, creating objects that were portable, informal, and humorous. Sacco, introduced by the Italian company Zanotta in 1970s, attacked the modernist creed of form and structure. This invertebrate bag of synthetic pellets, affectionately called the bean bag chair, became an indestructible symbol of youth, endlessly remade by subsequent generations. Meanwhile, green-minded designers like Victor Papanek sought technological simplicity in products that could be made by anyone from everyday materials. Victor Papanek's book Design for the Real World (1974) tried to restore design's moral rectitude while rejecting its artistic aspirations.

The theory and practice of simplicity suffered in the 80s, when it was mistaken for 'high-tech' luxury or blanketed over by post-modern historicism. Simplicity made its startling re-entrance in 1993, when Renny Ramakers and Gijs Bakker launched Droog Design and turned around the international discourse of design. They presented a collection of objects that used materials in a direct and unidealized way. These new objects used ordinary industrial goods and humble materials in a manner that refuses to philosophize, transcend, or transform them. Rody Graumans's 85 Lamps (1993), a chandelier assembled from 85 factory-made fixtures with exposed electrical connectors, does not magically transmogrify its materials into something more grandiose. The lamps hide nothing, asserting their normalcy without apology. Tejo Remy's Rag Chair

Birdfeeder

Paolo Ulian
2002
31,5 x 17 x 5,5 cm
poplar wood

Double walled tumblers

**Arnout Visser,
Erik Jan Kwakkel
1997
porcelain, hollow
Ø 6 x 9 cm**

Heat insulation between
hands and hot drinks is
guaranteed by the mug's
double walled structure.

128 Pantone mugs

Onkar Singh Kular
2003
bone china with sprayed glaze finish
Ø 7 x 9 cm

The colour of a mug could
be an indication of the
kind of coffee or tea you prefer.

Porcelain lamp

Dick van Hoff
1997
Ø 23.5 x 16 cm
porcelain

Stool

Richard Hutten
1994
beech, PVC coating
50 x 50 x 40 cm

(1991), a bundle of rags bound with steel strapping tape into the shape of a chair, is an archive of over-consumption that conceals neither its origins (nor its destiny) as refuse. In these projects, the dense massing of anonymous materials comments on industrial accumulation and waste.

From its inception, the Droog Design collection has included objects for the bathroom, the first domestic zone to let equipment show itself more or less directly. By the early twentieth century, consumers had accepted the smooth, unadorned surfaces of metal and porcelain appliances as part of a new domestic hygiene, allowing the bathroom to become a place where the sculptural geometries of modernism could feel at home. Objects from Droog's early collections amplified the utility of the bathroom by stripping away its pretensions of luxury and purity. Dick van Hoff's Tap 'Stop' (1995) is a faucet assembled from the sort of standard plumbing parts normally installed behind walls or inside utility closets. His stitched washbasin (1996), made from felt soaked in resin, replaces the aesthetic of the hard and shiny lavatory with a bladder-like form whose presence is base, bodily, and imperfect.

A different mode of simplicity asserted itself in the Function tiles (1997), which embedded a new range services into the ceramic grid of the typical bathroom. Extruded tiles become a shelf; vented tiles become a grille; sliced and folded tiles become towel hooks; a red tiled cross with a drawer at its intersection becomes a medicine chest; and so on. The tiles, designed by Arnout Visser, Peter van der Jagt, and Erik Jan Kwakkel, construct a network of possibilities rather than a singular object, offering specialized plug-ins for the standard software package of the home.

This disappearance of things can be seen in recent Droog projects as well. Hotel Droog, an installation for the Salone del Mobile, Milan, 2002, was staged in an existing hotel, where designers inserted elements over a several-day period. Some gestures were purely graphic, as when a group of graduates from IM Masters, Eindhoven, con- verted a public stairway into a gym by applying graphics to each riser, announcing the number of calories one might burn during ascent. This project—as resistant to metaphor as Droog's first objects—provided an interface for an existing structure, exposing an economy of ordinary use.

In Milan 2003, Droog's 'Your Choice' installation took the form of a store, replacing the singularity of objects in a typical gallery display with profusions of (nearly) identical things. Each project called attention to small, sometimes immaterial differences among items in a series. Onkar Singh Kular's 128 Pantone mugs were sprayed in minutely adjusted shades of tan. The difference was barely perceptible from mug to mug, but apparent across the field of objects, as in the combined impact of pixels on a screen. Several projects created under the brand banner 'United Statements' spoke to the arbitrariness of economic value, from t-shirts imprinted with the message 'Out of Fashion:

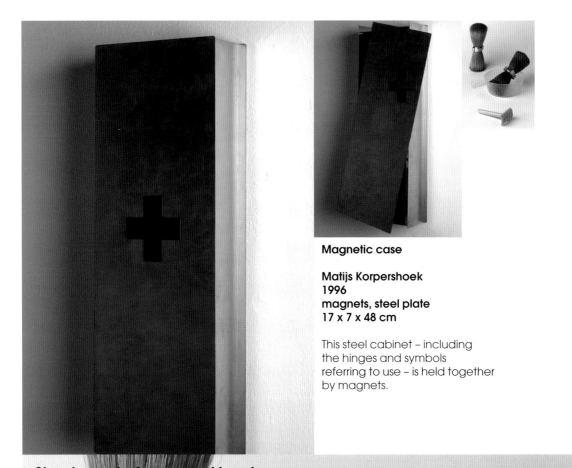

Magnetic case

Matijs Korpershoek
1996
magnets, steel plate
17 x 7 x 48 cm

This steel cabinet – including
the hinges and symbols
referring to use – is held together
by magnets.

Shaving set of razor and brush

Dick van Hoff
1996
PP, pig's bristles
4 x 4 x 12 cm

Lamp 'Wirelight'

Johee Lee
2004
EL-wire, epoxy resin,
standard 60 W light bulb
various sizes

New technology makes it
possible to employ both the wire
and the light bulb as a source
of light. The wire and the lamp's
filament run seamlessly into
one another.

Repacked

Niels van Eijk,
Mirjam van der Lubbe
2005
polystyrene foam, shrink wrapping,
bubble wrap
40 x 40 x 40 cm

Stool entirely made of materials from
the world of packaging. Sitting becomes
more comfortable the more packaging
material is added. From the Value for
Money project.

Jan Melis
1991
brass, terrazzo
100 x 100 x 250 cm

Dish mop

Gijs Bakker
2004
steel, foam
25 x 8 x 4.5 cm

Dish-washing brush made out
of a brightly coloured foam ball
clasped between the arms
of a steel fork. Turns doing
the dishes into a cheerful activity.
The separate spare balls make
nice toys too........

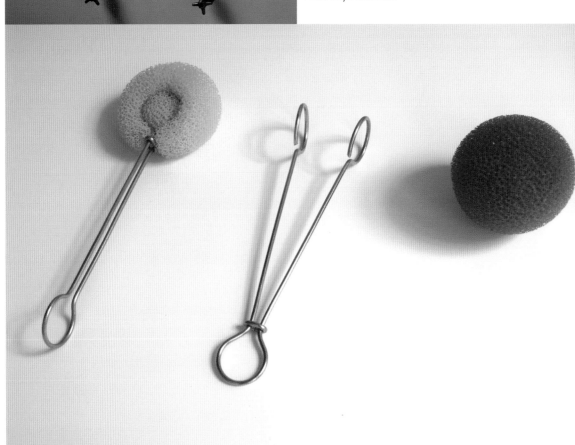

Tap 'Stop'

Dick van Hoff
1995
copper tubing
18 x 10 x 28 cm

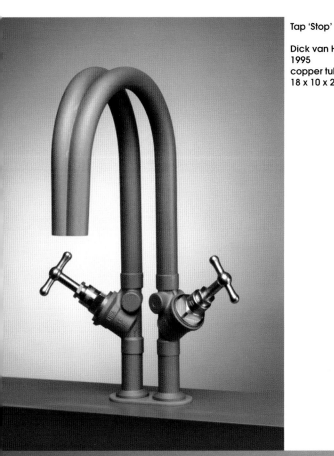

Chandelier '85 lamps'

Rody Graumans
1993
85 bulbs 15 W,
standard fitting, dimmer
Ø 60 x 100 cm

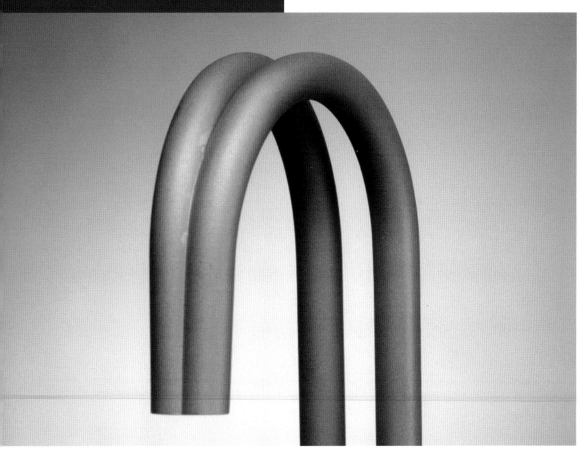

Han Koning, Louise Maniëtte,
Tarmo Piirmets, Jet Vervest
2002
self adhesive
pictograms in situ
various sizes
Picture: Hotel Droog 2002

Sticky lamps

Chris Kabel
2002
PVC, fluorescent light 6 W
18 x 25 x 7 cm
Picture: Hotel Droog 2002

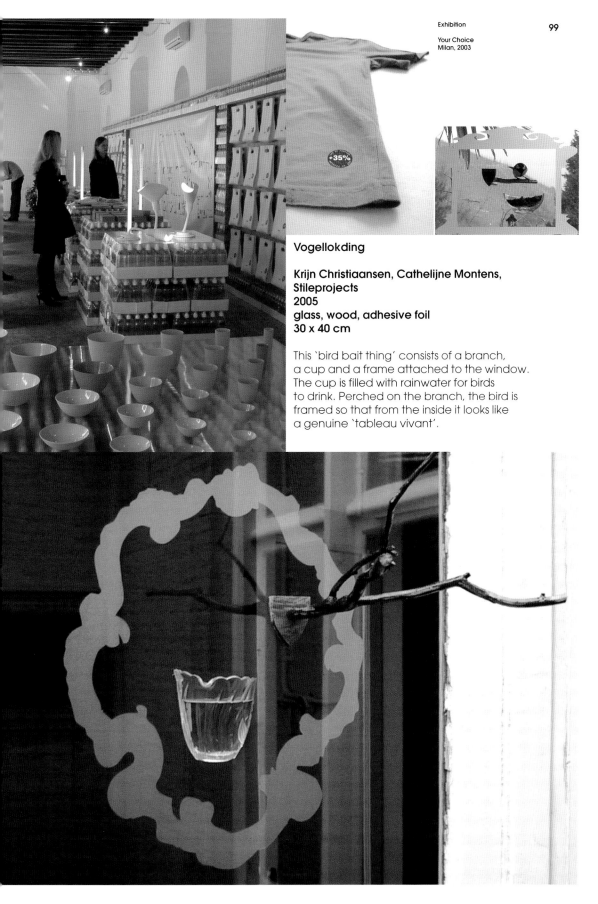

Vogellokding

**Krijn Christiaansen, Cathelijne Montens,
Stileprojects
2005
glass, wood, adhesive foil
30 x 40 cm**

This 'bird bait thing' consists of a branch,
a cup and a frame attached to the window.
The cup is filled with rainwater for birds
to drink. Perched on the branch, the bird is
framed so that from the inside it looks like
a genuine 'tableau vivant'.

Orange box cupboard

Hugo Timmermans
1991
red cedar
100 x 46 x 210 cm

35% Markup' to a group of identical synthetic felt bags marked with different prices. Vincent de Rijk created a set of bowls in 54 (slightly) varied sizes, each drawing its unique status from the overall series. Such projects shift attention away from the physical specificity of the object towards its place in a system of values.

Simplicity is a theme across the history of the Droog Design collections, but it is neither consistent nor absolute. In the first days of Droog, simplicity yielded objects of such astonishing density as Remy's Rag Chair and Graumans's 85 Lamps. That compacted archeology, that concentration of goods at a focused point of use, has now become diffused across environments of communication and exchange.

Soft knob

Ed Annink
1992
soft PU
Ø 7.5 cm x 8.5 cm/
Ø 12 x 14 cm

Change your view

Emmy Blok
2002
self adhesive translucent foil in situ
various sizes
Picture: Hotel Droog 2002

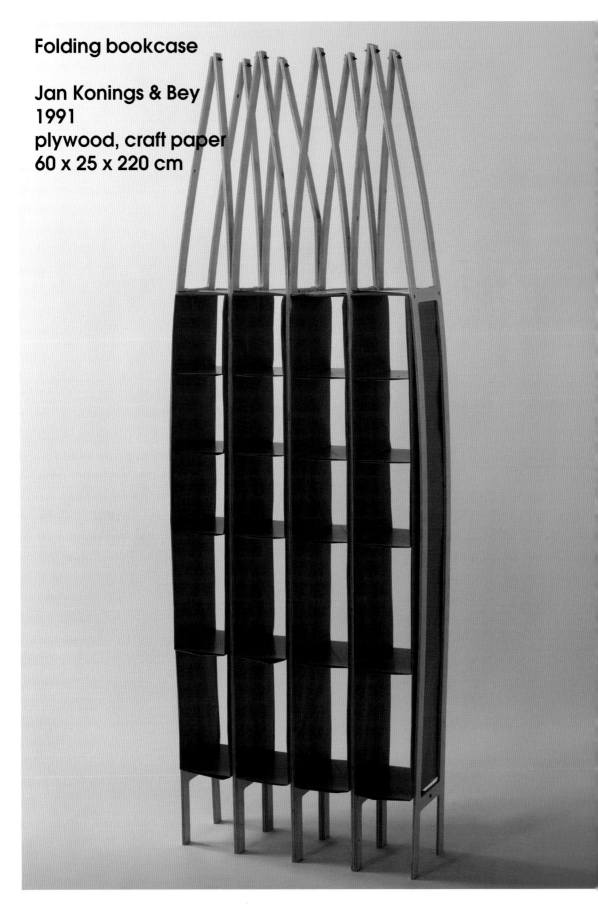

Folding bookcase

Jan Konings & Bey
1991
plywood, craft paper
60 x 25 x 220 cm

Free range kitchen

Ton Matton / Schie 2.0
2001
wood, metal and other material
various sizes

The kitchen functions free of any
infrastructure by deploying
environmental techniques aimed
at self-support such as water
purification, composing and local
energy. For example, the fridge
is cooled by a block of ice kept in
one of the drawers.

irony

Droog products reflect our culture in a critical way with a little twist. Sometimes they express a cynical comment.

Bench 'the cross'

Richard Hutten
1994
beech, PVC coated foam
120 x 200 x 75 cm

The bench was made for a fair in Italy together with the swastika shaped bench 's(h)it on it' to comment on the political situation in that country.

Flower bulb packaging 'Bolle box'

Andreas Möller
1994
compressed cow dung
8 x 8 x 8 cm

The idea is to sell the Dutch manure
surplus to tourists

Bench 's(h)it on it'

Richard Hutten
1994
steel, MDF
110 x 110 x 75 cm

irony

Ed van Hinte

Free-lance writer, editor, designer
and design teacher

Many Droog Design designs bring a smile to the face of everybody, well, almost everybody, who sees them. This happened from the very beginning. A lamp consisting of 'milk bottles', a book chest made according to the 'construction principles' of a book were recognized as new views on design, because they had some twist. Eibert Draisma made lamps and coffeemakers that 'behaved' and moved and were cute. But they consisted of carefully chosen old parts of various kinds that didn't get any attention before.

So what was going on here? To clarify the effect we have to creep into the dark and dangerous grottos of explaining humour, a quest not recommended to anyone who prefers the comfort of the absence of doubt.

In the case of Draisma's objects what you see is junk, but what you recognize is a funny animal. That is what causes the cheerfulness. It is not the simple registration of the object you see, but rather the understanding of certain implicit intentions that may be different from or opposed to the apparent meaning. It is where we enter the realm of irony. Irony presupposes understanding the invisible.
Suggesting humour is extremely difficult. In typed language, especially since the coming of age of email and SMS messages, the habit sneaked in of clarifying the feeling behind words with so-called smileys, combinations of punctuation marks that can be read as pictograms of facial expressions. They ought to be forbidden :-), because they are the pornography of alphanumeric code. Jokes and emotions should never be explained. Either you get them or you don't.
Yet in language meaning can be fooled around with, because reference is indirect. You can say: 'There is no snow at the South Pole.' An object, on the other hand, in the first place is always what it is. It is more difficult to lie with design. Still a product is able to tell something, comment on existing situations, by playing with expectations in terms of colour, materials, texture, context, or even just the name. Meaning emerges in our minds, from what we know beforehand as participants of the culture we live in.

Claudia Linders
2003
dress made of used
design labels
66 m ribbon

Owners of clothes from top
brands were requested to
replace the label by an
'Unlabeled' one. The original
labels are used to create a
long ribbon to make a dress
from.

A designer can use his creations to transfer meaning, but there is always the intriguing risk that the observer misunderstands. This can happen in two slightly tragic ways. The first kind is when a more often than not inexperienced designer, without any hidden agenda, creates something straightforward that nevertheless seems to suggest much more. Consequently observers perceive layers of meaning that were never supposed to arise. The result can be that the work of this designer has an inspirational quality that others have yet to explain to her or him.

The second is just the opposite: a designer may have attempted to express something that later is misinterpreted or not understood at all. The flower bulb packaging 'Bolle Box' by Andreas Möller had this effect on some people. Whereas the cubic box, made out of smelly dry manure strongly suggested logistic efficiency, - put a bulb in a box 'edible' by plants, and then put them in the ground together to get your flourishing tulip -, it was by no means proposed as a realistic solution to some existing manure surplus problem. Yet some people commented that this idea wouldn't work.

More generally Droog Design was perceived as presenting ironic alternatives for a more sustainable society, especially in the beginning when many of the products incorporated used materials and familiar shapes. The designers, however, had different considerations, based mainly on esthetics.

Since irony presupposes a certain amount of knowledge, the clues offered work differently for different audiences. The inner circle of the design community becomes a partner in ironic crime concerning design itself. Designers perceive reflections on their own work, use of materials, conventions of production, the essence of beauty, comments on the context within which they create new things. The general public may be more inclined to be surprised by the ingenuity of ideas, like the clever use of the ability of oil to float on vinegar, or the exploitation of drinking glasses to create a doorbell. It is a familiar kind of irony that the late Achille Castiglioni, for instance, was a master at.

In recent years the emphasis in Droog presentations has shifted from mere product design towards lighthearted reflection on culture itself. They presented Claudia Linders' project 'Unlabeled', in which the designer challenged owners of clothes from renowned fashion brands to (carefully) undo the valuable label, give it to her, and replace it with her 'Unlabeled' one. She then sewed all the famous labels together to form one long ribbon to make a dress out of. The project succeeds in challenging the perceived value of famous labels in a sympathetic way. Cultural comment can be a bit more difficult to chew. In 2003 Simon Heydens of United Statements did a project in Milan selling T-shirts with stickers on them to announce temporary price increases of sometimes as much as 70 percent. Some prospective buyers just didn't see the irony.

If irony gets more angry it turns into cynicism. At Droog Hotel during the Milan furniture fair, itself a feast of irony, where all visitors had to get a special passport in which they

**Video 'Sit down Gentlemen –
respect the cleaning women!'**

Floris Schiferli
2002
video 3 minutes loop DVD
80 x 130 cm projection in situ
Picture: Hotel Droog 2002

Men wishing to make use of
the toilet are requested in this
video to answer nature's call
in a seated position. Images of
a hard working cleaning lady
call on the guest to contribute
to keeping the toilet facilities
neat and clean.

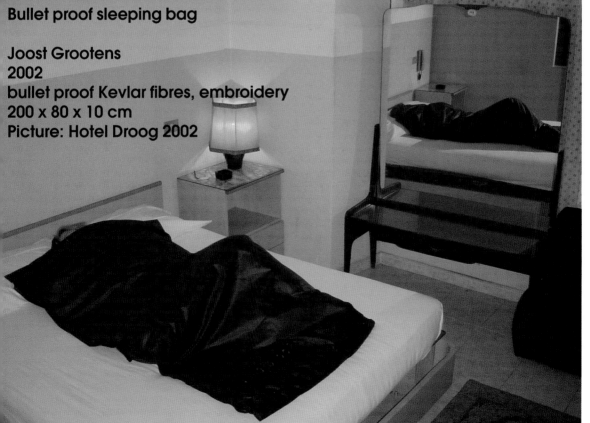

Bullet proof sleeping bag

Joost Grootens
2002
bullet proof Kevlar fibres, embroidery
200 x 80 x 10 cm
Picture: Hotel Droog 2002

could get a stamp for every product they had seen, Joost Grootens presented his Bullet Proof Sleeping Bag. Cynicism can evoke biting reactions. Richard Hutten experienced that in 1994 when he made two benches for the Abitare il Tempo fair in Verona, Italy. It was election time and the fascists had good prospects, which he didn't like. So he rather naively made one bench, called 'S(h)it on it', in the shape of the swastika and the other, 'The Cross', became a Catholic cross, because the Pope had collaborated with the fascists. There were some disturbed reactions, since the benches have no way of telling whether they are in favour of what they are symbolizing. Later on, at a different occasion, a German visitor cut the words 'nie wieder' in the fascist bench. Hutten decided to clarify this statement and cut it a little deeper, just to make sure that nobody would misunderstand his own intentions. Irony no doubt is an important means to attract attention and make a clear statement, but the author had better make damn sure that it is the right kind. For in that case design can raise questions that feed doubt that in its turn may open new ways to thinking. That is the secret of irony and it is a secret that shall never be revealed to anyone.

50 differently priced bags

Simon Heijdens, United Statements
2003
white synthetic felt, sticker
30 x 10 x 40 cm

Absolutely the same bag ,
but a different price.
On what basis do people choose?

NEXT Architects
2003
MDF, linen
90 x 40 x 200 cm

This bookcase has been
filled up with important
literary works that together
provide a high cultural
status. This literature will be
gradually replaced by the
personal choice of the user.

body language

The ability to touch is at odds with the tendencies in our society towards de-materialization, which makes it extremely relevant today. Structure, texture, relief and elasticity act to arouse the sense of touch.

Soft lamp

Arian Brekveld
1995
white soft PVC, 25 W
Ø 10.5 x 22 cm

With this lamp the old PVC
technique has acquired
a new use. The cord almost
melts into the soft shade.

Flexlamp

Sam Hecht
2004
silicone
Ø 33 x 22 cm

Lamp 'Superpatata'

Hector Serrano
2000
100% natural latex, salt,
11 W bulb
Ø 25 x 25 cm

Soft washbowl

Hella Jongerius
1997
Soft PU, metal
25 x 15 x 20 cm

Pushed washbasin

Hella Jongerius
1997
soft PU
40 x 25 x 20 cm

The wash basin is based on the idea
of turning non-form into form through
the qualities of the material. A basic
shape is pushed inwards, which make
the top fall over. Differences in the
thickness of the skin determine its final
shape.

Saar Oosterhof
1996
Soft PU
24 x 24 x 1,4 cm

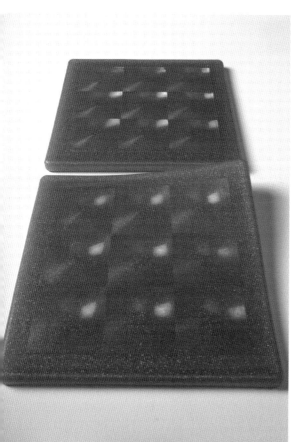

Moonwalk carpet

Elske Revelman de Vries
2003
100% wool, soft PU
180 x 120 x 8 cm

body language

Marieke Sonneveld

Part time researcher at the Delft University of Technology, Faculty of Industrial Design, Department of Design Aesthetics, director of research and consultant company Tactile Affairs.

Imagine touching Arjan Brekveld's soft lamp. The first thing that strikes you is that no words whatsoever spring to your mind. Maybe all you come up with is a mere mental sound: 'Hmmm…', or just a big yawn of indifference. Apparently there is no frame of thought to make your understanding of tactile experience more profound. This may start to be a real problem when in product design tactility becomes an aspect of aesthetic experience.

For visual beauty designers have a sophisticated vocabulary. They are not likely to simply proclaim that they are going to design 'something that looks good'. More refined notions about lines, proportions, colour and meaning are part of the common design idiom. Likewise, designing 'something that feels good' is a poor statement, offering little grip, and therefore resulting in cliché's of making things soft, smooth, or with kinky textures and floppy protuberances, without a clue as to why this may be appropriate. Tactile experience emerges from physical interaction with our surroundings, from our bodies and parts thereof being in contact with other material objects. Considering the lack of tactile terms a few lines earlier, it is quite surprising that words to describe personality traits of people specifically refer to material properties in the world of touch. The examples are easy to find and numerous. A person can be warm, cool, weak, soft, harsh, flexible, stiff, supportive, rough, smooth, sticky and, naturally, a pain in the ass. These individual idiosyncrasies may literally be perceived during physical interaction, for instance in the case of shaking hands with somebody. We all recognize the sissy boy in his boneless hand, or the insensitive dominator if he offers a painful nut-crushing experience.

When you touch an object you get a certain sense of identity in exactly the same way. If it feels cold, soft or flexible, it is not only literally perceived as such, but simultaneously experienced metaphorically as having a cold or soft or flexible personality. Objects are just like people. They have a meaningful body language that can be experienced as such once you've set your mind to it. Following that line of thought,

Bathroom mat

Hella Jongerius
1993
soft PU
60 x 40 x 4 cm

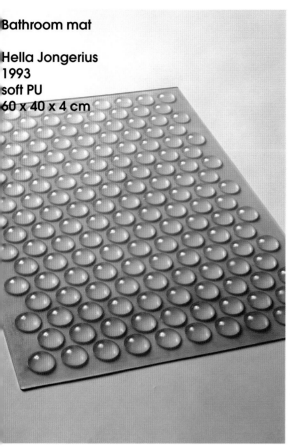

there appear to be appropriate and more abstract personality traits to describe how objects actually feel: there are objects with mean edges, a friendly rounding, or haughty squareness.

Recognizing personality in things may be due to the fact that, contrary to what is often believed, physical interaction with objects is not simply a matter of human skin touching surfaces. For in actual fact you use your entire body to feel an object as a whole. When touching a product, you manipulate, squeeze, push, weigh and caress it, and by doing so, it reacts. It touches you back.
The personality of objects, the way they make themselves known to you, is not only understood by their material properties, but also by their behaviour when they react.
When you move, you have many different reasons for doing so. Man-made movements are meaningful (although they don't necessarily have to be conscious). That may well be the reason why the movements of objects are perceived as part of their personality. It seems as though the object wants things to happen too.

This has striking consequences. Objects we have to touch serve as tools, or supports, or toys. During interaction, they appear to make clear to what extent they are actually willing to cooperate. They show whether they are doing what they are supposed to or just following their own pigheaded plans. Some scissors do precisely what you want, whereas others seem to prefer to take a bend to the left and damage your paper. Skateboards, skis, bicycles, computers and particularly cars are other examples of objects that seem to have a will of their own, and they are loved for that, as they challenge you to tame them. Mutual misunderstanding can also result in rage that breaks windows every day.

Some objects just don't want to be used. Think of stiff heavy mountain boots, that seem to say 'I don't really like mountain walks at all' when they are literally clinging

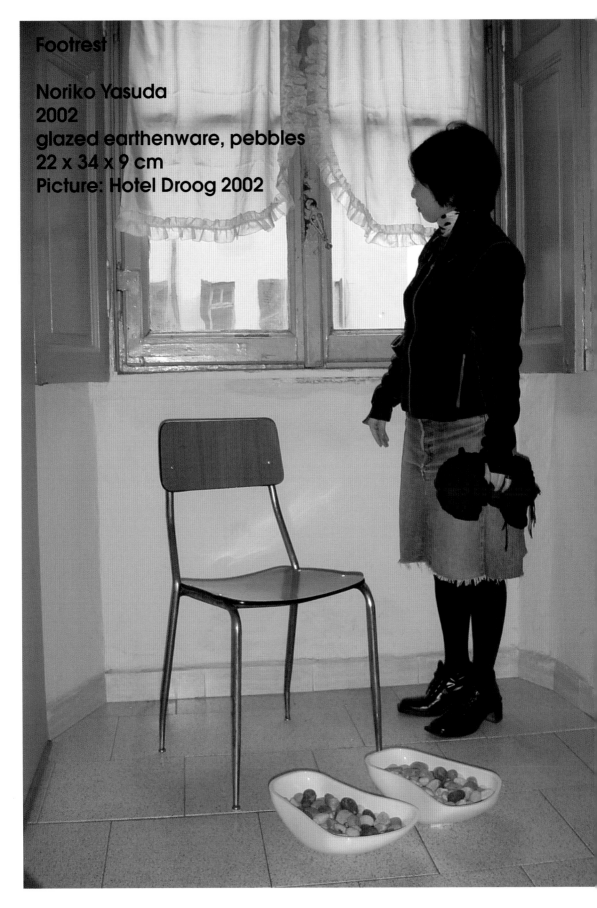

Footrest

Noriko Yasuda
2002
glazed earthenware, pebbles
22 x 34 x 9 cm
Picture: Hotel Droog 2002

o your feet. Their behaviour is entirely unlike that of nice bouncy, flexible running
shoes that enthusiastically jump up and down with you when you're warming up.

Apart from the actual, functional use of objects, there are other reasons to touch them,
the main one being curiosity. Ever since childhood people touch objects to explore
them, to get to know them, or just to make sure that their eyes are not deceiving
them. All 'Please Do Not Touch' signs in shops, museums and galleries stand witness
to the lack of appreciation of this human instinct to touch. Like people, some objects
just seem to love to be explored. And when you do fulfill their desire, velvet cushions,
marble sculptures, and objects with loads of interesting buttons all behave differently.
Sometimes when exploring things, we like to feel right through the surface, to arrive
at the core of what we are touching.
Objects that hide behind their outside are always frustrating, especially when we want
to play with them. Luckily some objects simply love to play along. A rubber band
never wants to be put down again, and the mechanism in ballpoints doesn't seem to
let you stop clicking.

Beauty is in the eye of the beholder, but it is tactility that completes the personality of
things. Think of your bathroom floor, made of natural, but cold and rigid ceramic tiles,
arrogant and distant in the way they greet your bare feet in the morning. Lacquered
wood might feel slightly warmer, but is still a bit stiff, and occasionally supplies you
with a splinter in your toe, just to nag you. Next, imagine your feet being welcomed
by the sensual touch of Saar Oosterhof's PU tiles: they truly love to love you.

Soft toilet

Arnout Visser, Erik Jan Kwakkel
2000
blue silicon, white ceramics
122 x 122 x 220 cm

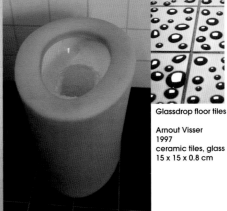

Glassdrop floor tiles

Arnout Visser
1997
ceramic tiles, glass
15 x 15 x 0.8 cm

Braille door handle

Joost Grootens
1995 / 2000
stainless steel
13 x 6 x 2 cm

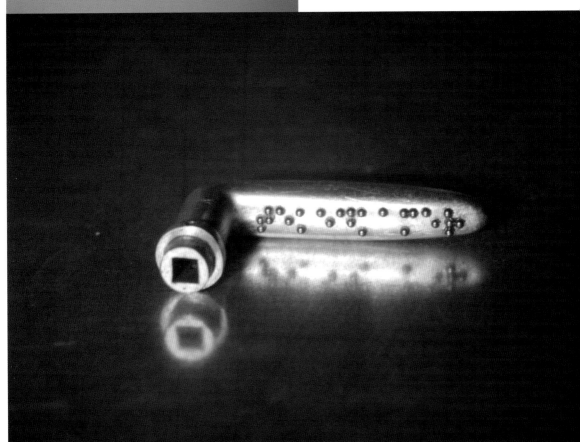

expe-rience

The experimental aspect, placed centre stage in the 80s play an important part in the Droog collection. But with Droog it proceeds in another direction. Not because products send out a wealth of visual stimuli but by way of a subcutaneous level that proves to pleasantly excite the spectator.

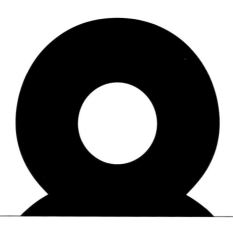

Share fence

NEXT Architects
2001
wood and other materials
200 x 200 x 4 cm

expe-
ience

d van Hinte

ree-lance writer, editor, designer
nd design teacher

It is impossible to determine exactly who started it, but towards the end of the Nineties, out of the blue, 'experience' became a catchword. It may have received extra attention because of the 1999 book 'The Experience Economy', by James Gilmore, but he already had a reason to write his publication, so obviously something had been going on around the notion of 'experience' already. It was the consequence of a combination of consumers spending more money then ever on immaterial commodities, such as entertainment and travelling. There was also the unprecedented explosion of Internet use, characterised by new issues like 'the feel of a website', meaning the quality of its interactive flow. The common factor in these phenomena is a certain time interval, long or short, during which a scenario of perceptions and actions takes place. Arnout Visser's Salt Glass literally shows the flow of time after one has salted the egg.

ne fate of important words in business and trade is that for a couple of years hey become the most crucial property of everything undertaken: 'It's experience tupid!'. Brands, for instance, were no longer just symbols representing ideal worlds around product consumption. Instead they were to become artificially linked o experiences that consumers could undergo, often literally, like the Heineken xperience, consisting of 3000 square meters of beer brand exhibition in the old eineken brewery in Amsterdam.

Jaturally experience also became a buzz word in design. The Design Academy in indhoven, for example, started in 2001 Funlab, a new Masters course in experience lesign. The implications all depend on the way in which experience is defined. Generally it is a set of consecutive visual, but sometimes also auditive and tactile perceptions that are so memorable that it becomes a fixed association in people's minds, vhenever part of the same circumstances occur.

Pinball machine 'Lucky cat'

Nari Tadaaki
2003
ceramics, wood, metal
84 x 104 x 130 cm

Active table cloth

Sanne van Engen
2002
print, textile
86 x 180 cm

A pinball machine offering music instead of profit

Arnout Visser
1995
glass
Ø 7.5 x 28 cm

Soft wooden floor

Front
2005
vinyl, recycled foam, canvas
3 cm x various sizes

A seemingly wooden floor is made of cheap material, with a soft layer underneath. Walking on the floor provides a surprising sensation.

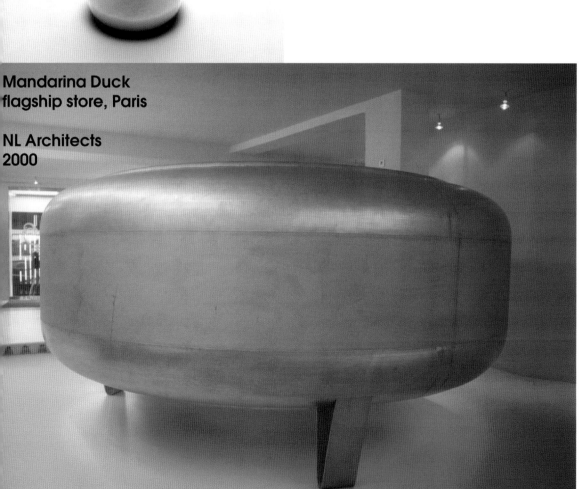

Mandarina Duck
flagship store, Paris

NL Architects
2000

Experience design is by no means a new phenomenon. It is after all experience by which people have always got to know the things they use and the services they consume. Producing experiences is a natural part of all results of creative activities. Designing a table or a car, writing computer software or a book, preparing a meal, directing a film, they all implicate experiences for those using or consuming them. Some take a few seconds, others may take days. Often they involve some form of interaction.

The 'proclamation' of the 'new' opportunity to plan and design experiences did bring about one important difference with the past way of thinking: experience became a far more explicit factor, and in many instances all other properties of products and services as well as the need for materialization itself, became subordinate to it. It meant a shift in emphasis. To illustrate it rather bluntly: designing a knife turned into planning the experience of preparing a sandwich. This turn in design thinking brought about a challenge to explore new areas of problem solving.

Droog Design also surfed the wave of experience design. It did so from the very beginning, unknowingly and implicitly at first. The first presentation of Droog Design in Milan together with Pastoe in 1993 was a particularly fine example, because it showed unprecedented and therefore memorable views on the discipline of design itself. It meant nothing less than an experience in the mind of observers, of ideas and inspirations about what products could be, in addition to what they already were.

**Mandarina Duck
flagship store, Paris**

**NL Architects
2000**

do swing

Thomas Bernstrand
2000
stainless steel,
existing lampshades
11 x 48 x 50 cm

do break

Frank Tjepkema,
Peter van der Jagt
2000
porcelain,
silicon rubber
Ø 15 x 34 cm

It was the shock of the new. Since that first occasion Droog's exhibitions have acquired a reputation based on experiences undergone by visitors.

There are many kinds of experiences. Being impressed by an unexpected presentation is just one of them. Droog Design has explored some others. The first attempt at explicit experience design was the project 'do create', in which a number of designers were asked to design a product for KesselsKramer's brand 'do' that users had to appropriate through an action they had to undertake. In this way they could personalize their newly acquired possession and enforce the feeling of individual ownership by experience. The presentation, with products and photographs of 'owners' undergoing the appropriation experience was quite successful. Yet with hindsight one can wonder to what extent the respective items on display can truly be considered experience design. The objects had already had their treatment, visible in the pictures. Spectators could see them as illustrations of acts they had to imagine themselves performing with the products. They could purchase one of their own of course, and try it at home, but not all the presented examples were strong enough as products in the long run. One of the better ones is 'do swing' by Thomas Bernstrand, a double lamp shade that you can hang on and use for physical exercise. Its experiential quality is in the fact that, apart from being pleasantly weird, you can keep on using it and develop interesting lamp exercise skills over a longer period of time. It is not, like some of the other 'do' things, something that you appropriate once and then leave it at that.

Another interesting more recent experience exploration was 'Me, myself and you' in 2001. It had a more social nature in the sense that the designs were meant to facilitate interaction between humans. Especially the bench 'Come a little bit closer' by Nina Farkache, a bench with round seats 'floating' on glass marbles, worked quite well, because people spontaneously started to play with it rolling on the marbles and bumping against each other's bums, without having to imagine different contexts or environments or even the looks of the object. It simply did what it was supposed to do and presented users with a new kind of freedom to experiment.

The best example of experience design no doubt is the interior of the Mandarina Duck flagship store in Paris which NL Architects made for Droog a year earlier. It is a combination of different experiences of wandering around in a shop, selecting items and trying on clothes. A revolving spiral staircase confuses your sense of direction, garments are hidden behind metal and handbags exposed and clamped against the wall with rubber bands. Synthetic reed serves as a strangely romantic privacy curtain to get dressed behind. The store clearly demonstrates growing experience in designing experiences to be remembered. For experience is about memory.

Bench 'Come a little bit closer'

Nina Farkache
2001
stainless steel, glass marbles,
lacquered MDF
68 x 406 x 43 cm

The discs can slide over the
rolling marbles. Sitting becomes
play and play can bring people
into contact.

Bowls 'Reinventing Rituals'

Michelle Huang
2002
porcelain
various sizes

These rice bowls are based on the idea
of reinventing Chinese rituals. Leaving
some food means respect for the host,
that's why the bowl has got an extra
pocket. The bowl with the handle refers
to the habit of lifting the bowl when
eating rice.

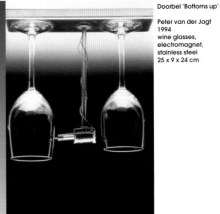

Doorbel 'Bottoms up'

Peter van der Jagt
1994
wine glasses,
electromagnet,
stainless steel
25 x 9 x 24 cm

Oil and vinegar set 'Salad Sunrise'

**Arnout Visser
1990
pyrex glass
Ø 4 x 18 cm**

This table object is based on
the phenomenon of oil floating
on vinegar

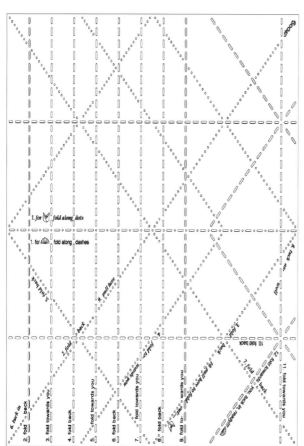

Napkin 'Twofold'

Chris Kabel
2004
100% trevira
42 x 42 x 0.3 cm

A napkin with two different laser-cut patterns
to fold two classical dinner table pieces,
a fan and a mitre. The holes and lines together
make up a luxurious lace-like pattern.

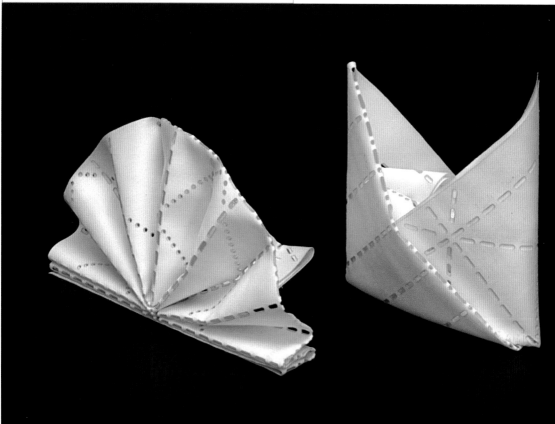

Table cloth 'Tableau'

Maurice Scheltens
2005
photogram printed on cotton
280 x 130 cm

Table cloth decorated with the
shadows of a table arrangement,
projected on the cloth by a
photogram technique. More than
merely casting shadows of plates,
dishes and glasses, the cloth tells
a story and reflects the atmosphere
of the dinner through shadows
of what might have happened at
this table.

Napkin 'Before and After'

Chris Kabel
2004
100% trevira
42 x 42 x 0.3 cm

A napkin inspired by the idea that it is neatly
folded before dinner and is carelessly folded after
dinner. The fold-lines of the napkin before and
after dinner have been integrated in the napkin
and cross each other like dotted lines. This design
proves that decoration can be used in a functional
way. The holes of the lace serve as fold-lines.

Ventilator Blow

Wokmedia
2005
nylon SLS
Ø 24 cm

Fan without a switch to turn it on or off.
You blow the little fan to turn on the main
propeller, then stop it with your finger
to switch it off.

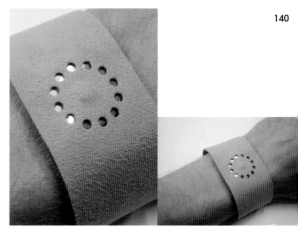

Watch 'Moment Maker'

Jason Ifkathar
2005
cloth, LED clock
3.5 x 22 x 0.35 cm

This colourful timepiece is a reflection of
the way we, as human beings, tell time to
each other. We tend to round up time
to the closest subdivision of the 12 hour clock.
By pressing its single button, two different
coloured LED's are illuminated, indicating the
time with an accuracy of five minutes.

endless contamination

Amidst the tendencies to miniaturize and substract, additive designs are seeing the light of the day. In their search for new ideas, forms and typologies, designers tie functions together. In certain respects design-practice is more material-minded and realistic than ever.

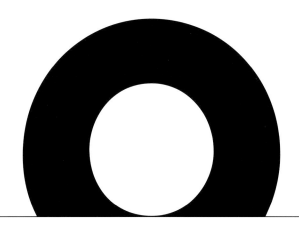

Socket light

Paul Hessels
1990
sandblasted glass
7 x 15 x 12 cm

endless contami- nation

Ole Bouman

Writer, designer and editor in chief
of Archis, a magazine for architecture,
city and visual culture.

One of the most famous aesthetic concepts is the figure-ground motif. Based on the universal dialectics between foreground and background, one is able to single things out, to isolate. And now, suddenly, there is a work that is both figure and ground at the same time, a hybrid. A wallpaper lamp (by Jaap van Arkel).

One of the most famous practical concepts is one that differentiates between conditions and preconditions. Before you instill a value, a meaning or an idea, you need to set up a situation in which this can happen. So, first you need a socket before you can have light. And now, suddenly, there is a work that is both precondition and condition: a hybrid. A Socketlight (by Paul Hessels).

One of the most famous architectural concepts is the fence, demarcating mine and yours, inside and outside, public and private. With a fence one is bound to make a difference, a division between threat and protection. And now, suddenly, there is a work that is both demarcation and trait d'union: a hybrid. A Table Tennis fence (by Next Architects).

Look at the Droog items that are displayed in this section. Look carefully, not just at their appearances, at their shapes, at their patterns, at their volumes, at their forms, at their colours, at their physicalities, no, look at them as acts. As efforts. As endeavors. As projects. As strategies. Eventually: consider design as a strategy to change the world. Well then, how do these items change the world?

By means of an hybridization of the mutually exclusive. Socle and sculpture, sedation and activitation, function and ornament. An endless contamination of what used to be separated. Look at the table cloth (by Saar Oosterhof), the tablechair (by Jurgen Bey). These works seem to be born out of an allergy against any mental, practical or theoretical classification of reality. This is a change of the world indeed.

Not by pure invention. Not by pure creation. Not by designing from a tabula rasa. Not by projecting, scheming, cold intervening. Not by overruling the existing. Not by giving birth to the new, not by the shock of the new. Works like the Clotheshanger Lamp (by Hector Serrano) or the Function Tiles (by Arnoout Visser, Erik Jan Kwakkel en Peter van der Jagt) do not represent such an essentialist world view. And still, the world is changing.

Kokon furniture 'table-chair'

Jurgen Bey
1999
PVC coating, existing furniture
various sizes

The opposite of essentialism is existentialism. Life is not dead. Life is a flow, not an object; so to change it, you don't need a hammer, you need intelligence. Not brawns but brains. Clearly, design can be a lateral work; it is about mixing, it is about adding, it is about emulating, com-plementing, tranforming, shading, mutating, modifying, blurring, sampling, photoshopping. And yes, hybridization. What comes into exis-tence is neither pure nor solid nor universal nor modern nor dictatorial. What happens is a soft-ening of form to the extent that it may flow over to other forms. Concepts that seek their overlap with other concepts. But what is more important is that hybridization is not just a matter of fusing opposites, merging extremes, or mixing dialectics. It is much stranger than that. This hybridization is about making things compatible that previously simply didn't have anything to do with one another. They permit us to overcome a regime of understanding that we are normally enslaved by. Form, size, taste, function, concept, theory, paradigm, all these mental tools that once were invented to keep the world together, are being unraveled into a thesaurus of elements which are ready for recombination. They tend to break free from premises, rather than submit to rules.

Of course, we have been familiar with this approach for quite some time now, also known as non-design. But in the case of the objects under consideration the most convincing is probably that this whole blasphemous approach doesn't lead to anar-chy as a goal in itself, but to a new integrity of form and a new gravity of object, to a universe for which this little article is way too short to find the natural laws.

Table tennis fence

NEXT Architects
2001
wood and other materials,
ping pong net
200 x 200 x 4 cm

Clothes hanger lamp

Hector Serrano
2002
acrylic, fluorescent
light 11 W
41 x 22 x 5 cm
Picture: Hotel Droog
2002

Matwalk

Paolo Ulian
2002
cotton
59 x 95 x 3 cm
Picture: Hotel Droog 2002

Wallpaper lamp

Jaap van Arkel
2000
wallpaper, resin,
metal frame, 15 W
43 x 13 x 11 cm

Hot spot pain relief
T-shirt

Susanne Philippson
2002
cotton, cherry stones

Tablecloth with bowl

Saar Oosterhof
1998
soft PU
160 x 160 x 14 cm

Table-chair

Richard Hutten
1991
beech, white lacquered MDF
60 x 60 x 71 cm

French Flemish glasses

Wieki Somers
2004
crystal
Ø 6.2 x 19 cm

Reasoning that the French prefer wine, whereas the Flemish people drink more beer, Wieki Somers created a new glass that serves both purposes. The glass was made within the framework of Lille 2004, emphasizing the location of Lille near the French-Flemish border.

5 glass containers

Wieki Somers
2004
crystal
various sizes

Two different classic glasses are melted together to become a single container.

Function tiles

Anout Visser, Erik Jan Kwakkel,
Peter van der Jagt
1997
ceramic, other materials
15 x 15 cm, depth variable

Function tiles

**Anout Visser, Erik Jan Kwakkel,
Peter van der Jagt
1997
ceramic, other materials
15 x 15 cm, depth variable**

form follows process

Designers show an interest in self-organizing processes. While society embraces total control, designers are forfeiting part of theirs. While genetic mani-pulation takes strides forward and cosmetic plastic surgery gains even wider application,

they let nature take its course. Products may – or better, still – must wear out and perish. Nature may overrun the product or even cause it to disappear altogether. Designers also employ the production process as a form-giving force. The factor time plays a key role in this pro-cess-based approach.

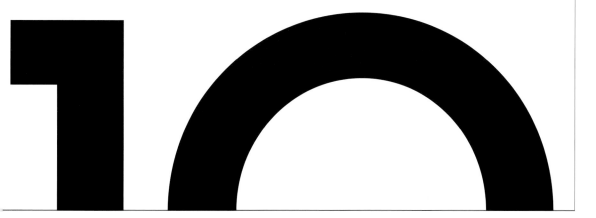

Richard Hutten
1997
rotation moulded soft
and hard PU
55 x 28 x 35 cm

form follows process

Ed van Hinte

Free-lance writer, editor, designer
and design teacher

This ongoing struggle between humans and their own marvellous and ever growing ability to automate things is absolutely fascinating, especially if you look at it from an historical perspective. Allowing machines to gradually take over control over work we hate to do seems a simple matter of technological evolution at first glance, but the consequences in terms of acceptance, experimentation and straightforward mistakes are manifold. The trouble can be found in the amount of control designers of all kinds can bear to delegate.

The first control dilemma occurred in the esthetics of the products that machines make for us. It is the insoluble matter of authenticity and expression. A tarnishing observation is that in this respect all progress starts as imitation of the known. The first cast iron columns, designed in the 18th century, were made in various, but always familiar looks. And the first synthetic plastic, celluloid, was developed as a replacement for ivory in the middle of the 19th century. More recently, in the middle of the 1980s, the first animated virtual environments were made to coincide with real ones.

But also there was always the odd visionary who went back to the question: So what do we have here? Pure functionalist architects and designers recognized the potential of industry to produce for the masses, provided form was kept simple. In 1964 Gerrit Rietveld himself said: 'The charm of artisanship lies in the sketchy and the laborious; the charm of machine work lies in the perfect design that puts high demands on designers. We see these new forms as guides of social justice' (Ed van Hinte, Wim Rietveld; industrieel ontwerper, 1996). This austere attitude was challenged, both because the market was not really interested in this ideal of perfect simple forms and because mass production developed into a far more flexible system than the purists had foreseen. A current marketing notion is mass individualization. As a consequence software is replacing the mould as the 'master definition' of products, and changing software is far easier than changing hardened steel counter forms. Change is easily

Cultivated crack

**Simon Heijdens
2004
earthenware, glaze
various diameters**

Earthenware with
an extra layer applied
under the glaze with
a decoration of a flower
or branch. In contact
with warm liquid the
decoration stands out
in crackle.

Front
2005
wood
1 m x 1 m x 50 cm

Table with a pattern
made by animals:
insects ate out the
design of a wooden
table.

automated these days, or even randomized if required. It is now possible to produce different cars of different brands on one single production line. Almost twenty years ago experiments with different laser cut decorations in steel table objects were already being done. The basic idea was that every individual should be able to choose his or her own custom made product. However, computers remain instruments of control.

Droog Design has demonstrated attempts to unchain the process of production and to make it work in such a way that differences arise by themselves, to a certain extent by challenging the paradigm of industrial perfection. Hella Jongerius had a hard time convincing the man who controlled the machine that produced her polyurethane rubber vases that she didn't want the gas bubbles to be removed from the transparent material because they provided a lively look. Richard Hutten produced the first version of his Bronto children's chair from an uncontrolled mixture of colours of material, which provided the product with a charming roughness. The principle behind Dick van Hoff's 'Extrusion Plates' is a bit like that, except that in this case the mixing machine that spits out porcelain mass is fed with two colours. Interestingly, in the same period that these products were first put on display, Marjan Unger, head of the Applied Arts Department of the Sandberg Institute, bought simple plastic plates just like it on her travels through Africa.

The choice of technology can become more poetic and far reaching. For the Oranienbaum project that partly had to do with the exploitation of a park, Jurgen Bey came up with a bench that is extruded from fallen leaves and mowed grass in the park with a special machine. Depending on the season a piece of bench will always look different and it simply rots away over time.

Shape can be trusted to the whims of production too. Most experiments have been executed by firing ceramics. The B-Service of Hella Jongerius is probably the first successful attempt to make ranges of items that are all different because of the chosen firing temperature. Frederik Roijé invented a slightly different varying procedure. He designed a porcelain lamp shade that is not really stiff enough to withstand the heat in the oven. As a result all the lamps end up in a different state of collapse. Because of that they all have a different personality. Another variation was carried out by Erik Jan Kwakkel for the Central Museum in Utrecht. He used existing porcelain moulds, but filled them with an amount of material, that normally would have been considered insufficient. The result: all mugs and plates have a different edge. This kind of experimentation appears to be quite inspiring. Design students are still trying to find their own version of bringing back coincidental beauty to industrial processes.

A kind of control that has to be avoided, simply because it is a nuisance, is the one that excludes users from using products. It is the kind in which a number of functions have been combined, to be controlled by one, not very intelligent, computer system. It can happen for instance, that a video projector can only be put to work if the curtains in the

Extrusion plates

Dick van Hoff
1997
white and blue porcelain
Ø 25 x 2 cm

A series of plates in which no
two are the same by mixing
two colours of clay in the
extrusion machine and letting
the machine dictate the
change of colour.

Service 'B - set'

Hella Jongerius
1999
porcelain with
imprints
various sizes

room are closed. 'Curtains open, no image', the programmer had decided and there
is nothing anyone else can do about it. Droog Design has commented on the lack of
computer system transparency in its installation System Almighty, which was included
in the exhibition 010101 in the San Francisco Museum of Modern Art in 2001. Visitors
could scan any bar coded item they had on them to switch on four out of forty electric
devices for a few seconds, but only the trial revealed which combination was triggered
by a certain barcode. The behavior of people who tried it appeared to be somewhat
strange. With a bar code they could turn on a lamp, a vacuum cleaner, a saw and
what have you, something they could easily do at home. Yet in the museum it became
a special attraction, because control became enigmatic. People even stood in line
for it. We like to be uncertain, as long as all is safe. This holds true for designers too. They
like to experiment with the degree to which they can let things happen by coincidence,
but in the end they are always in control of the limitations. That is why the struggle will
have no final outcome.

Jurgen Bey
1999
hay, resin, leaves, bark
200 x 72 x 78 cm

Fatlamp

NEXT Architects
2004
glass, fat, cork,
25 Watt G9 lamp
Ø 16 x 31 cm

Lamp with a light source that is hidden in fat.
Turning the light on starts an intriguing process: you
can see the structure of the fat slowly melting and
the light becoming gradually brighter. You can feel
the lamp warming up. A typical example of slowness
highlighted in Droog's 2004 Go Slow presentation.

Spineless lamp

Frederik Roijé
1997
porcelain, 100 W Halogen bulb
23 x 18 x 33 cm

Paraffin table

Timo Breumelhof
2000
white paraffin
60 x 60 x 100 cm

Oranienbaum candy

Martí Guixé
1999
poplar wood, candy, orange seed
15 x 5 x 1 cm

One eats the candy, plants the seed and
puts the stick next to it as a warning that
in 20 years' time itwill have grown into a tree.

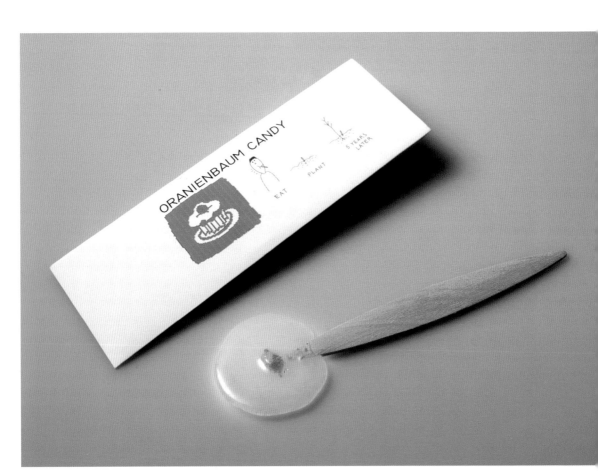

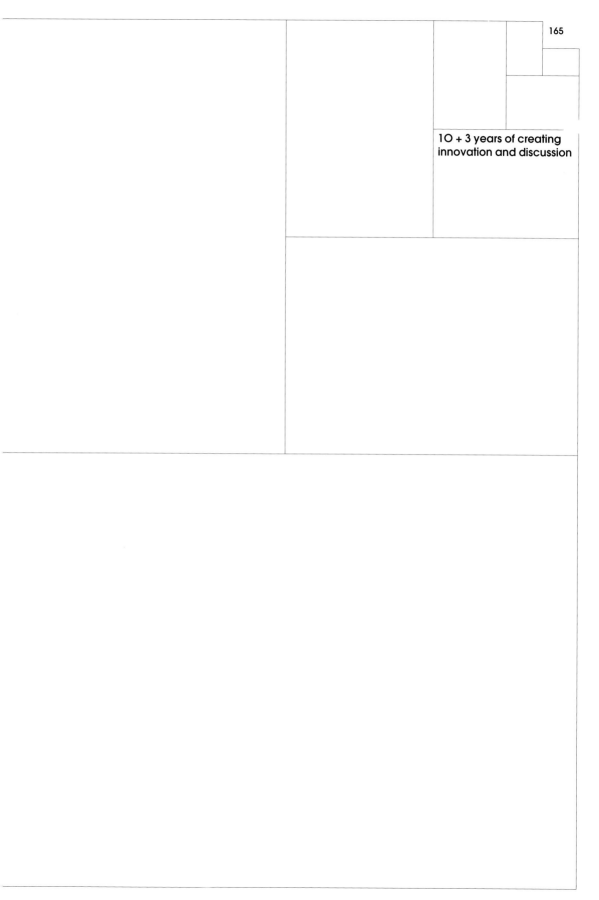

10 + 3 years of creating
innovation and discussion

1993

Presentation Milan, April 20-25

Ed Annink, Gijs Bakker, Jurgen Bey, Eibert
Draisma, Piet Hein Eek, Richard Hutten,
Djoke de Jong, Jan Konings, Gert-Jan Leusink,
Tejo Remy

Chair with holes

Gijs Bakker
1989
maplewood
44 x 43 x 78 cm

in vi ta ti on

Pastoe & Droog Design

April 20-25 1993
10.00-21.00
Via Cerva 14, Milano

Andrea Branzi will give an introduction
Wednesday 21 April at 18.00
cocktail offered by the Consul General
of the Netherlands

with thanks to:
The Netherlands Design Institute
European Design Center Eindhoven
Akademie Industriële Vormgeving Eindhoven
Incontri Culturali Olandesi (ICO)

Italian Designer Andrea Branzi opens the first presentation of Droog Design. In his speech he labels the products 'protestantism'. It is not clear whether he means this in a positive or a negative sense.

Gijs Bakker and Renny Ramakers haven't got the faintest idea of what things will be like, when in April 1993 they are present in Milan as a duo for the first time. They have rented a space in a beautiful old house filled with antique furniture at the Via Cerva, where the Dutch manufacturer Pastoe has been presenting itself for years. Financial support has come from a number of Dutch institutions. Bakker and Ramakers show sixteen products under the name 'Droog Design'. Among them are the milkbottle lamp and rag chair by Tejo Remy, a cupboard made of scrap wood by Piet Hein Eek, the chair with holes by Gijs Bakker and two cupboards by Jan Konings and Jurgen Bey.

To their surprise the attention these products get is overwhelming. The most striking reaction is recorded in the French paper Liberation. After complimenting a number of famous designers, the author of the article concludes that the award for the most spiritual 'savoir-vivre' should go to an unknown group, called Droog Design.

The Dutch word droog means dry

Architektur
& Wohnen Heft 4/93 augustus/september 1993

Gar nicht dröge: „Droog Design

Erfrischend und umweltbewußt ist das junge Anti-Design aus Holland.

*D*roog Design" (trockenes Design) nennt sich eine Gruppe niederländischer Designer, die mit Recycling-Materialien, trockenem Witz und Spiel-Lust durchaus plausible, neue Produkt-Ideen entwickeln. So wurde zum Beispiel eine aufklappbare Bibliothek präsentiert, die – wie Bücher – nur aus Pappe, Papier und Leinwand besteht, oder ein Tisch, auf dem man mit Kreide schreiben kann. Zuerst in Mailand im Pastoe-Showroom vorgestellt, werden die Droog-Taten bald auch in Deutschland zu sehen sein.

Gestapelte Schirme, Tischleuchte von Marcel Wanders.

Tafel-Tisch mit einer Schicht aus Schultafelfarbe von Djoke de Jong.

Bücherregal von Jan Konings und Jürgen Bey.

Milchflaschen-Lampe von Tejo Remy.

Garderobe von Jan Konings – eine theatralische Veranstaltung.

14

1994

Presentation Milan, April 11-17

Gijs Bakker, Jurgen Bey, Eibert Draisma, Rody
Graumans, Richard Hutten, Djoke de Jong,
Hella Jongerius, Jan Konings, Gert-Jan Leusink,
Tejo Remy, Henk Stallinga, Hugo Timmermans,
Marcel Wanders, Arnout Visser

Droog Design

catalogue

Gijs Bakker and Renny Ramakers decide to
continue their activities. On January 28th 1994
they establish the foundation Droog Design
with the objective of 'international promotion
of Dutch design which fits within the concept
of Droog Design and establishing international
contacts for production and distribution.'
In the same year they start to cooperate with
Teake Bulstra who has just set up the company
DMD, specialized in development, manufacturing and distribution. Among the first products
that DMD takes into production are the milkbottle lamp by Tejo Remy and the oil and
vinegar set 'Salad Sunrise' by Arnout Visser.

For the second time Droog Design is present in Milan, in the space Internos – Donna Elissa which is shared with DMD and Cor Unum, another Dutch company. Dutch designer Ed Annink has designed the installation. Together with the Netherlands Design Institute, Droog Design publishes a modest catalogue, designed by Joseph Plateau. It contains the Droog Design Collection, now consisting of 27 products.

For the second presentation in Milan Droog has invited Le Cri Neerlandais, a group of young fashion designers to do a fashion show as part of the opening ceremony. It is held outdoors on a little square in front of the space, in which Droog is presenting. The audience gathered there does not react enthusiastically. Italian men in the audience criticise the models whom they consider ugly. Among the fashion designers is the duo Viktor & Rolf.

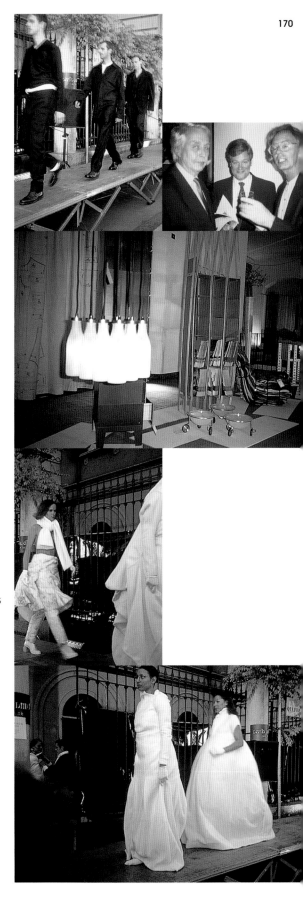

Gijs Bakker
Die Brille verrät viel:
Die Suche nach der
reinen, minimalistischen Form führte
Gijs Bakker zum
kreisrunden Loch. Der
52jährige Designer
und Begründer von
»Droog Design«
doziert an der
»Akademie für
industrielle Formgebung« in Eindhoven

Erstmals macht
niederländisches
Design international
von sich reden. Mit
humorvollen Entwürfen der Gruppe
»Droog Design«

Die Leichtigkeit der Holländer

Aktive Auseinandersetzung
mit der Vergangenheit: Die
mit Löchern durchsetzte,
einfarbige Tapete »**Peep
Show**« überdeckt nicht wie
andere Tapeten alles
Vorhandene. Sie integriert
die ehemaligen Wandfarben
in den Raum der Gegenwart,
gewährt kreisrunde
Erinnerungen

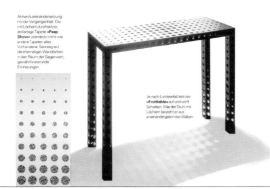

Je nach Lichteinfall liebt der
»**Fruittable**« auf und wirft
Schatten. Wie der Stuhl mit
Löchern besteht er aus
aneinandergereihten Stäben

The bench 'S(h)it-on-it' by Richard Hutten, representing a reverse swastika, unleashes a storm of protest by German visitors. During the opening party the words 'nie wieder' are scratched into the bench by someone in the audience. Richard Hutten decides not to restore the object, because as he feels this inscription contributes to a good understanding of his creation.

Gijs Bakker präsentiert Objekte, die ohne Gebrauchsanweisung auskommen. Erfrischendes Design mit deutlichem Konzept, neuen Funktionen oder Materialanwendungen. Bei jedem Stück ist die beschwingte Mentalität der »trockenen Designer« zu spüren. Ihr Hauptproblem: In den Niederlanden existiert keine Möbelindustrie wie etwa in Deutschland.

Ein engagierter Designer gehört zu den Suchenden, zu jenen, die sich nicht mit einer Form zufriedengeben und Perfektion

anstreben: Daß der Holländer Gijs Bakker vor einigen Jahren das kreisförmig herausgeschnittene Loch für sich entdeckt hat, heißt noch lange nicht, er habe das Ende seines kreativen Weges erreicht. »Ich wollte eine minimalistische Form als Ausgangsbasis«, erklärt der gelernte Industrie-Designer, der früher Kaffeemaschinen (Moulinex), Straßenlaternen, öffentliche Fahrradständer und Schmuck entwarf. »Ich gehe ins Material hinein«, sagt Gijs Bakker über seine jüngsten lochdurchdrungenen Arbeiten. Tische und

Stühle, Lampen, Tapeten und Vasen. »Ich bohre niemals ein Loch, ohne mir Gedanken über seine Plazierung, Größe und Funktion gemacht zu haben.« Bakker hat die Buchstaben seines individuellen Design-Alphabets definiert, aber noch keinen Text damit geschrieben. Erst einige Worte.

Der minimalistische »Fruittable with holes«, so nüchtern er auch dastehen mag, geht spielerisch mit Licht um. Er läßt es durch die unterschiedlich großen Öffnungen in Tischplatte und Beinen scheinen und wirft

LEONARDO 4/94

E 4668 E   1 1994   moebel interior design   MD 1, 1994

md

Moving lamps 'Sinus' & 'Cosinus'

Eibert Draisma
1990
rejected material
60 x 20 x 60 cm

DROOG DESIGN'S DRY WIT

Droog Design operate a discreet style of subversion by redefining the familiar. Michelle Ogundehin sees how fun becomes form

The Dutch national character is traditionally perceived as reserved and retentive, expressing a collective identity of measured sophistication. Where design is concerned, this means furniture and products that are clear in concept and form and executed with an uncomplicated palette of materials. Even in the 1980s, when excesses of style and decoration dominated everything everywhere else, for the Dutch it was restraint as usual. And now that "non-designed" design is the aesthetic of the moment, the Dutch are back in fashion.

Yet beneath any calm exterior there can lurk a sharp sense of the absurd –

although if there is a Dutch subversive underbelly, it's pretty discreet. The aptly named Droog (dry) Design, however, is a group of young furniture designers who have built on this firm cultural foundation but gone on to inject it with an increasing element of the wayward, to reveal both virtuosity and humour. Translating fun into form, Droog have brought about a wealth of innovation and fresh interpretations, with an increasing use of ready-mades also provoking contextual re-readings as the use and surface of familiar objects are redefined. Rody Graumans has created a chandelier from 85 light bulbs, their flexes caught in a knot of plastic connectors; a chest of drawers by Hugo Timmermans has an orange-box feel, but is manufactured in immaculate red cedar lending it an air of serenity.

Dutch designers' customary use of simple materials is sustained: wardrobes are constructed from aluminium framing swaddled in bleached cotton; maple plywood upstands support the packing paper shelves of a bookcase; and laminated floorboards are fashioned into a storage tower. Conceptual clarity is unchallenged, exemplified by Arnout Visser's Salad Sunrise Pyrex oil and vinegar holder. It's designed around the two liquids' differing specific gravity so only oil or vinegar will come out at one time.

Simple pieces with a twist abound in the Droog repertoire. There is Djoke de Jong's elegant but spare MDF Drawing Table which comes sized for children or the kitchen and is finished in blackboard paint, giving its title added significance. Gijs Bakker's Peepshow wallpaper constructs a dialogue between old and new as perforations in the paper of varying dimensions expose the layers beneath. A narrative discussion is invoked by Tejo Remy's chest of drawers entitled "You Can't Lay Down Your Memory", made of a selection of old drawers of various formats and origins, each newly housed in a solid maplewood surround, clustered together seemingly at random and held fast by a broad webbing band. His Milkbottlelamp (which you can see at

Space in All Saints' Road, London W11) is formed by sandblasting twelve standard milk bottles and suspending them in a grid on adjustable cables to hover just above the floor.

Remy's work is representative of the new aesthetic, and a larger movement in the Netherlands. Verging on the sculptural, his pieces accommodate an individuality particular to the nature of the found objects and the purchaser. His Rag Chair, of compressed clothing secured by steel strips, actually encourages customers to provide their own worn out garments to be incorporated into the seat.

Droog Design aren't afraid of humour, but clarity and simplicity are still the key factors. Left, above left and top centre: Tejo Remy's Rag Chair, Milkbottlelamp and You Can't Lay Down Your Memory drawers. Top left, Marcel Wanders' Set Up Shades lamp, and right, Arnout Visser's Salad Sunrise. Above: Gijs Bakker's stainless steel Vertical Holes candlestick

1995

Presentation Milan, April 7-11

Ed Annink, Jaap van Arkel, Eibert Draisma,
Martijn Fransen, Dick van Hoff, Richard Hutten,
Peter van der Jagt, Djoke de Jong, Hella
Jongerius, Andreas Möller, Henk Stallinga,
Hugo Timmermans

Dry Tech

Whereas Gijs Bakker and Renny Ramakers started by selecting products from the work of young Dutch designers, now they decide to stimulate new developments themselves as well as to create more coherence in their presentations. They start Droog's first project 'Dry Tech' in collaboration with the Laboratory for Structures and Materials of the Faculty of Aviation and Aerospace of the University of Technology in Delft. Curiosity about the outcome of a craftsman's approach towards new materials sets the project in motion. Designers are invited to experiment with high tech fibres. The clash between systematic scientific research and design experimenting turns out to be productive. Plastics with fibres are extremely strong but they also appear to have an unexpected aesthetic potential that deserves further exploration. Dry Tech is presented in Milan in 1996.

Presentation Milan, 1995

Exhibition / Kunsthal Rotterdam, December 2 - January 28, 1995/96

In 1995 Droog Design writes:

All attempts to draw up selection criteria for the Droog Collection are doomed to fail. Again and again we are faced with exceptions to the rule. We are not interested at all costs in humour, in environmentally friendly design, in re-using products and forms, nor do we have a specific interest in non-design or the implementation of simple materials and techniques. And yet these elements are always present in some form or another. In product one there may be more of element A and in product two more of element B, while in product three completely different features may be dominant.

Droog Design does not represent a style, but an image. Our time brings the image down on itself and therefore it will always be subject to change. The Droog collection is at right angles to the dominant culture of our highly technologized Western society, drenched in abundance. While the world around us is getting more and more complex and industrial systems seem to become increasingly abstract, Droog Design proposes simplicity and clarity.

As our market-oriented world seems to become increasingly superficial and new developments succeed one another with such tremendous speed that our culture seems to get trapped in mere consumerism, Droog Design represents content and the value of what is already here. In a society, in which so many products move about that the original design can hardly survive, Droog Design wants to show the richness of personal concepts. Now that 'design' has degenerated into style, Droog curbs styling and addition of features. It breaks with the established values of material use and shape.

But Droog Design does not hide from social reality. The themes dominating the design world at present are felt to be very relevant. There is no utopism. Droog is convinced that apparently opposite developments may in fact be parallel and the same source of inspiration. That is why we do not want to confine ourselves to traditional materials or production methods. We are interested in everything our technological culture has to offer.

It is interesting to see how the media picture Droog Design. Much of what they write makes sense. Very striking are the differences. Some value the multiplicity of ideas. Others look at Droog from an ecological perspective. Paola Antonelli, design and architecture curator at the Museum of Modern Art in New York, gives detailed comment on the production process of Rody Graumans' chandelier '85 lamps' in a Dutch television program: 'a process which is virtually harmless to the environment'. In the 1995 International Design Yearbook the French architect Jean Nouvel notices 'a strong element of ascetic non-design'. Droog Design is also often associated with humour. Another Jean Nouvel quote: 'Once again one of the designers from Droog Design has given the supposed straightforwardness a slight but witty twist'.

Intramuros, June/July 1995

DROOG DESIG
The L'avant-gard
Dutch Avant

*Banquette-table "The Cross",
design Richard Hutten.*

L'esprit de contestation est une qualité essenti lorsque l'on veut se démarquer, et le groupe d design néerlandais Droog (un jeu de mot sur "sec") n'en manque pas. Droog s'est fait conna depuis trois ans à Milan, à travers des exposit organisées dans des showrooms "off" du Salo Meuble. Réunissant un groupe de jeunes desi, des Pays-Bas, Droog est une initiative audacie utilisant des idées fortes avec des moyens sim Droog est une aproche originale en dehors de pays d'origine. Les objets, ici, interpellent le s tateur avec subtilité et ironie en élargissant u champ de créativité inattendu.

Droog Design a été initié par Gijs Bakker et Renny Ramakers, res ment designer et critique, tous deux très reconnus aux P Bakker, le "parrain" de Droog, designer le plus célèbre de bijoux dais, n'hésite pas à faire des incursions dans le mobilier, le design duits, le mobilier et l'éclairage urbain. Son travail permet de mie prendre l'attitude interpellante de Droog. A Milan cette année, il p une table à pied sphérique percé, développement de son "holes-pr projet des trous) en cours d'évolution. Précédemment, il avait p trous dans un siège en érable "Chair" (1989), pour alléger son po

Hollandaise
arde

*Rangement
design Hugo Timmermans.*

*A naturally wayward tendency is a fine quality to
have to get things to go your way, and the Dutch
design group Droog (a pun on the word "dry")
Design, possesses it in abundance. Droog have boldly pitched themselves into the foreground of the
Milan Furniture Fair through exhibitions held in
"fringe" showrooms throughout the city over the last
three years. Droog, a judicious selection of young
Dutch design talent, combines a strong idea or message with simple and crisply economical means.
Droog promotes a common mentality quite conspi-
cuous outside its home territory. Droog objects pene-
trate the viewer's conciousness on a much more subtle level, opening mental doors protectively shut to
overgrown, grand design statements.*

*"Milkbo
design '*

*D*roog design was initiated by curators Gigs Bakker and Renny
Ramakers, designer and writer respectively, both active on their home
territory with regular presentations of new creative ideas. Bakker, Droog's
"godfather", is the Netherlands's most famous jewellery designer, a hybrid
figure known for his forays into furniture, product design, street furniture
and lighting projects. His own work, essays on reinvention, providdes a good
insight into the questioning mentality of Droog. The Milan show this year
showed a pierced spherical-legged table, the latest incarnation in his evol-
ving "holes-project". Earlier, he drilled perforations into his 1989 Chair with
holes in maple to make it lighter by at least a third without affecting its
strength. Where the tension was the last, the perforations were the largest,
making the field of tension a visual feature of the chair's design.
   "What interests me is the fact that I'm not designing a shape but probing one. In literal terms I'm hollowing it out, but emotionally I'm probing it.
It gives me so much scope for ideas. I get inside it like a woodworm. Working
this way gives an object a much deeper meaning. As a result the viewer's
focus oscillates freely between the design's optical effect and the element of
experience. Bakker is not a designer who serves industry : he likes to main-
tain a sense of critical distance, working independently when he can. In
common with many innovative Dutch designers, his is a systematic approach where every element, even the smallest hole, has a reason for existing.
Similarly, going back to basics, Droog style, is a journey away from comp-
romise, self-indulgence and humorless uniformity, a mentality which
involves, a bit like Bakker's oh-so-holey chairs, a lightening up in tone and
in form in order to get a better focus.
   Whereas earlier Droog collections have emphasised the use of natural
materials and recycling, the newest range shown during this year's Milan
Furniture Fair focused on the original use of synthetic materials -soft polyurethane used to make tactile, floppy rubber "wobble" vases by Hella
Jongerius, which will be shown in MoMA New York's forthcoming "Mutant
materials" exhibition, the red painted foam block seat of a maple stool base
by Richard Hutten, an active exhibitor on the Dutch design scene, or even
Andreas Möller's tulip bulb case made of dried manure.
   Launched with the help of grants from various Dutch cultural bodies,
Droog design has thrown a host of original ideas concealed in an atmosphere free from narrow commercial constraints into the glaringly spotlit ring of
the commercial design world. The cryptic, occasionally disturbing (like
Richard Hutten's black four seater design, its arms in the shape of a swastika) and mostly less than obvious (Konings & Bey's artfully bandaged wardrobe from 1994) nature of Droog's droll pieces - a door bell made with
ordinary clear wine glasses, laundry and wastepaper bins made from bill-
board posters- naturally throws them open to accusations of art school postu-
ring. But Dutch design has traditionally melded art and design concerns in
an Intellectually confident and rigorous fashion, and the flow of ideas from
Droog washes over a rich seam of parallel and overlapping areas of human
interest.
   Tejo Remy, the star of last year's Milan exhibition, uses old drawers
(bound together in a cluster and evocatively titled "you can't lay down your
memory"), milkbottles and clothes from various origins combined to make*

●●●

*Chaise-table "Sit on it"
design Richard Hutten.*

Tous les objets présentés cette année, même ceux qui ne sont pas vraiment évidents, s'appuient sur une notion de fonction, libérée de "gestes" aussi vains que vagues. Certains sont tranquillement esthétisants, comme les carafes de verre de Ton Haas, ou les bahuts gris inclinés de Jaap van Arkel, qui rappellent d'une certaine façon la collection Progetto Ogetto de Cappellini. La fascination de Droog pour la résonance de l'objet utilitaire est particulièrement actuelle, et ses activités débouchent sur un commentaire très personnel sur l'utilité et l'ingéniosité dont on ne peut qu'apprécier l'allégresse, face à la prolifération du design minimaliste et fonctionnaliste.

Osés, intelligemment provocants, les objets de Droog se sont fait remarquer dans un Milan dominé par des fabricants prudents, anxieux avant tout de ne pas bousculer l'équilibre précaire de leurs mini-empires, après les sévères rebuffades infligées par la crise. Par ailleurs, sans se préoccuper de la naïveté et du refus de l'industrie qui prévalait dans le design européen des années 80, Droog, en s'assurant la collaboration de DMD (Development Manufacturing Distribution, de Voorburg) pour la commercialisation de beaucoup de ses projets (certains fabriqués par les designers eux-mêmes, d'autres par des fabriquants), a fait en sorte que ses travaux ne restent pas confinés aux murs blancs des nombreux studios de design et galeries néerlandais.

Ceci entraîne pour chaque projet quelques ajustements de matériaux ou de procédés de fabrication. Teake Bulstra, directeur de DMD, lui même diplômé en design, et qui a dirigé pendant plusieurs années la production et la distribution de Pastoe, a pris en charge la gestion de ce processus. Il croit fermement que les bonnes idées doivent aller de l'avant et se multiplier, et s'engager sans crainte sur le territoire de la distribution, en particulier à une époque où les consommateurs sont devenus réceptifs à un mélange d'esprit et d'économie. Ils recherchent autre chose que les formules standard d'Ikea, et ne sont certainement pas opposés à des objets quotidiens flirtant avec l'art : "L'œuvre doit être présentée au public dans sa totalité. Les vases doivent pouvoir aussi fonctionner comme vasque. Au cours du processus de réglage en vue de la production, on rediscute le concept. Mon rôle est multiple; je veux communiquer des idées sous forme de produits. Nous prenons tous les risques, mais je ne force jamais le changement. Par exemple, comme la table à dessin de Djoke de Jong est trop coûteuse à produire pour espérer être vendue, je lui ai demandé de réfléchir à une autre façon de la fabriquer".

Environ trente produits Droog sont disponibles (la lampe-bouteille de lait de Remy, présente dans 15 points de vente néerlandais, est la plus largement distribuée), et DMD monte actuellement un réseau d'agents et de distributeurs aux Pays-Bas, en Allemagne, Belgique, Italie, Danemark, Espagne, Autriche, Canada et Corée. En Grande-Bretagne, le showroom londonien de Tom Dickson, Space, stocke Droog. Space, comme Droog, se consacre également à la découverte et à la production de travaux originaux de jeunes designers, s'occupant de la recherche de matériaux, de la production, du stockage, de la distribution et du financement, ce que la grande majorité des designers n'aime guère faire ou ne dispose pas du temps pour s'y intéresser. Conscient des problèmes de communication qui se multiplient tout au long du processus de production, Bulstra rédige actuellement un protocole très complet pour faciliter ces processus de production et de distribution.

Texte traduit par Jacques Bosser

Rangements à tiroirs design Djoke de Jong.

Robinetterie Droog, Design

Photo Mario Pignata Monti

*Groupe de design néerlandais
Droog Design.*

new, fresh statements that subtly effect a change in focus in the viewer upon the world they occupy, even if it is just a momentary, wry smile. The humble rough and readiness of the found objects, frequently set in a systematic formation, reveals a cleaner underlying surface of ideas, like old skin sloughed off to reveal younger, less tired material. Droog will never be, nor does it present an air of needing to be, ubiquitous, but the small scale many Droog objects possess makes a serious proposition about the healthiness of easy-to-live-with wit.

All the objects shown this year, even the ones which don't quite cut it in terms of clarity, embraced a notion of function free from vague, vain gestures. Some were quietly ascetic, like Ton Haas's glass carafes or Jaap van Arkel's grey tilted cupboards, somewhat redolent of Cappellini's Progetto Oggetto collection. Droog's fascination with the resonance of utilitarian objects is particularly timely, and its activities arguably create a highly distinct commentary on usefulness and resourcefulness that the current proliferation of minimalist, functional design needs to keep it buoyant.

Gutsy and intelligently provocative, Droog objects stood out in a Milan dominated by cautious manufacturers anxious not to rock their already precarious mini-empires after the severe buffeting inflicted by financial crisis. Furthermore, instead of the naivety or back-turning towards industry prevalent in European design in the 1980s, by enlisting the collaboration of DMD (Development Manufacturing Distribution) in Voorburg for the commercial realisation of many of the designs (some of which are made by other manufacturers, or by the designers themselves), Droog can ensure that the work is disseminated beyond the white walls of the Netherlands's many design studios and galleries.

This entails some adjustment of the concept of each design, of the materials and making process, and Teake Bulstra, DMD's director, and a design graduate who spent many years directing production and distribution for Pastoe, takes charge of managing this process. Bulstra feels strongly that good ideas should go forth and multiply, entering boldly into retail territory, especially at a time when consumers have become receptive to a mix of wit and economy, wanting more than standard Ikea and keen, to have an art work-cum-design object and household artefact rolled into one neat package "the work should be brought to the public as a totality. The vase should also work as vases. In the adjustment for production there are discussions about the concept. My role is that I can do a lot of things; I want to communicate the ideas as products. We take all the risk, but I never force the change. As it stands Djoke de Jong's drawing table design is too expensive for commercial production, for instance, so I've asked the designer to build it in a different way."

About thirty Droog designs are currently available (Remy's milkbottle lamp is the most widely distributed, and is currently sold in about 15 Dutch outlets), and DMD's building up a network of agents and distributors in the Netherlands, Germany, Belgium, Italy, Denmark, Spain, Austria, Canada and Korea. In Britain Tom Dixon's Space showroom in London stocks Droog. Like Droog, Space is also dedicated to finding and producing fresh, original work by young designers, taking on the sourcing of materials, production outlets and stockists, distribution and the financing that the vast majority of designers do not relish, or possess the time to develop a taste for. Aware of the problems in communication that crop up in the production process, Bulstra's currently writing extensive protocols to make the production and distribution process as painless as possible.

Lucy Bullivant

The Museum of Modern Art in New York opens a museum café furnished with Dutch design items like Tejo Remy's milkbottle lamps and Rody Graumans' chandelier `85 lamps'. These Droog products are selected by Dutch design studio Opera who designed the interior.

1996

Presentation Milan, April 18-22

Plastics new treat
Arian Brekveld, Roland Buschmann,
Danny Fang, Martijn Fransen, Paul Hessels,
Dick van Hoff, Peter Hopman, Richard
Hutten, Hella Jongerius, Oval
+
Droog Design by DMD
Ed Annink, Arian Brekveld, Rody Graumans,
Paul Hessels, Peter Hopman, Peter van der Jagt,
Hella Jongerius, Konings & Bey, Tejo Remy,
Arnout Visser

The Droog Design presentation at Gallery
Internos during the Salone del Mobile in Milan
is visited by more people than ever before.
On the opening day enormous crowds are
gathering and the police has to be called
in to control the traffic outside the building.
Title of the presentation is 'Plastics New Treat'.
On show are the first results of the Dry Tech
project and a number of plastic products.
Among the products shown are Hella Jongerius'
knitted lamp and Marcel Wanders' knotted
chair, based on macramé of a braid consisting
of carbon and aramid fibres. The knotted
chair has now been added to the collection
of various leading museums and to the Vitra
collection of miniature chairs.
The exhibition unleashes a lot of discussion
among visitors. Their idea of Droog advocating
recycled and natural materials is turned
upside down.

Lampade Oval, design di Arian Brekveld. Si tratta di utilizzare la tipologia dei gonfiabili in PVC, approfittando della loro trasparenza. Si utilizzano lampade standard a luce fredda come quelle fluorescenti o le PL che conviene stiano sempre al di fuori della visione diretta.

Oval lamps designed by Arian Brekveld. The aim was to take the typology of PVC inflatables, making use of their transparency. The designer goes for 'cold' standard lamps like the fluorescent lamp or PL's which always need to be out of direct view.

Knitted lamp

Hella Jongerius
1996
PMMA, fibreglass
50 x 28 x 15

Hella Jongerius about her knitted lamp:
'It was quite difficult to find a knitting factory in the Netherlands that dared to work glass fibres. So I had to make all patches myself on the knitting machine. The bulbs press against the resilient glass cloth. That provides the lamp with a shape. The edges were reinforced with perspex. Because of its High tech background I kept the form as flat as I could. It looks a bit spacy.' (Eigen Huis & Interieur, November 1996)

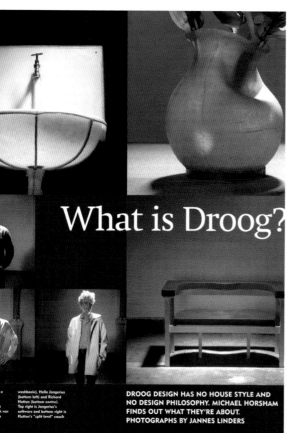

What is Droog?'
The media are puzzled:
'Is it a design group?
A company?'

Blueprint, October 1996

What is Droog?

washbasin), Hella Jongerius
(bottom left) and Richard
Hutten (bottom centre).
Top right is Jongerius's
software and bottom right is
Hutten's "split level" couch

**DROOG DESIGN HAS NO HOUSE STYLE AND
NO DESIGN PHILOSOPHY. MICHAEL HORSHAM
FINDS OUT WHAT THEY'RE ABOUT.
PHOTOGRAPHS BY JANNES LINDERS**

The Museum of Modern Art in New York organises a major exhibition on Dutch design, called 'Tresholds - Contemporary design from the Netherlands'. It inspires the museum to make a large number of new purchases. Curator Paola Antonelli selects some forty products, half of which are from the Droog Design Collection.

Bench 'the cross'

Richard Hutten
1994
beech, PVC coated
foam
120 x 200 x 75 cm

Richard Hutten's bench 'the cross' is added to the theatrical lobby of the famous Paramount Hotel in New York, designed by Philippe Starck.

Droog Design for Rosenthal During the Milan show Droog Design is approached by the German porcelain factory Rosenthal to take part in an experimental project to be presented in Milan the following year. This is the first time Droog Design is commissioned to design products. The aim of the project is to challenge porcelain's elegant and smooth image. Designers are selected and asked to develop various ideas around product use, texture, colour and production itself.

Cappellini launches knotted chair
The renowned Italian firm Cappellini introduces Marcel Wanders' knotted chair on the international market.

Cap 3, Autumn 1996

Marcel Wanders about the knotted chair: 'I wanted to make a product that doesn't look industrial, a design that shows that it is lovingly made especially for someone, with the same kind of aura as an old worn down wooden cupboard. Knotting is a technique with which you can achieve this artisan atmosphere.' (Eigen Huis & Interieur, November 1996)

1997

Presentation Milan, April 9-14

Dry Bathing
Ed Annink, Arian Brekveld, Roland Buschmann,
Paul Hessels, Dick van Hoff, Peter Hopman,
Peter van der Jagt, Hella Jongerius, Jan Melis,
Aukje Peters, Schoffelen & Van Meegen,
Arnout Visser

+

Dry Tech II
Dick van Hoff, Martijn Hoogendijk and Wiebe
Boonstra, Hella Jongerius, Konings & Bey,
Marcel Wanders

+

Droog Design for Rosenthal
Gijs Bakker, Dick van Hoff, Hella Jongerius,
Arnout Visser, Marcel Wanders

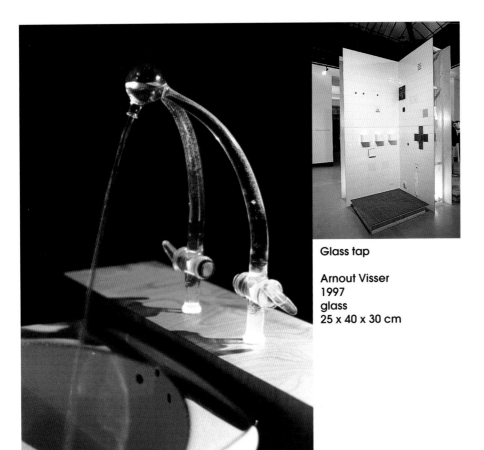

Glass tap

Arnout Visser
1997
glass
25 x 40 x 30 cm

Dry Bathing, new ideas for the bathroom Droog Design aims the arrows of its mentality at bathing. Like 'Dry Tech', this project is about overcoming the limitations of materials and discovering the potential of new functionality. In cooperation with DMD, Droog Design commissions designers to develop new ideas for the bathroom. The result is a large number of inspiring concepts for just about every bathroom product.

During the International Furniture Fair in Milan the products are shown in an installation designed by Ed Annink. In the entrance hall, the theme is set by Arnout Visser's glass tap, that visualizes temperature by colouring the water stream with light, red for hot and blue for cold. Among the products at the presentation is the waterfall shower by Jan Melis. Hella Jongerius presents two different washbasins of rubbery polyurethane.

Dry Tech II After the presentation in Milan, the project 'Dry Tech' continues and further results are shown in Milan, in a presentation named 'Dry Tech II'. Hella Jongerius makes fibre stools, using the technique of coiling high tech fibre. Marcel Wanders makes a table of Swiss lace reinforced with epoxy resin and Jan Konings and Jurgen Bey turn old chairs and tables into strange cocoons with an elastic synthetic spraying material that is normally used to wrap airplanes and army vehicles when they're not in use.

Design Report 7, 1997

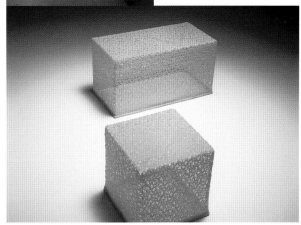

Lace table

Marcel Wanders
1997
swiss lace, resin
30 x 60 x 30 cm
prototype

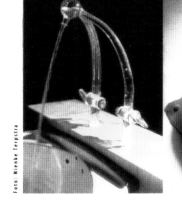

Foto: Nienke Terpstra

Foto: Marcel Loerismans

In **„Glass Tap"** von **Arnout Visser** steigt das heiße und kalte Wasser durch rot und blau beleuchtete Zuleitungen aus Glas auf.

Hella Jongerius setzt ihre Experimente mit Polyurethan fort. Auf die Vasen und eine Badematte folgen die **„Soft washbowls"**.

Ungewöhnliche Materialien für gewöhnliche Dinge

Wrap chairs

Hella Jongerius
1997
polymer
36 x 36 x 45 cm

Rosenthal Both Droog Design and Rosenthal show the results of the Rosenthal project during the international furniture fair in Milan. Although Rosenthal decides not to take any of the designs into production, many of them now belong to the Droog Collection and some will be produced in series later. Fashion designer Karl Lagerfeld wants to buy the Rosenthal pieces but this is not possible: 'I'm a big fan', he admits in the New York Times. 'Droog Design is the spirit of modernity. It is non-design and unpretentious … Can you imagine, Rosenthal didn't produce any of it? I wanted everything and all I could get was the porcelain lamp. I might send a complaint.'

Arnout Visser, Erik Jan Kwakkel
1997
porcelain
8 x 9 x 5,5 cm

The New York Times does a portrait of Droog Design for the issue of April 17. The newspaper quotes Murray Moss, owner of Moss design store in SoHo: 'Droog is all about material, not form. They take something simple, like a plain white tile and make a big deal out of it. That it's just a prototype isn't the point. The point is that every-one who looks at it goes 'Ah''.

FILM
The New Line studio pays a price in going big. **15**

TELEVISION
WNET raises a record $70 million and creates its first endowment. **15**

BOOKS
Two Bogart biographies go past the tough veneer to the tough core. **20**

The New York Times

H⊙me

THURSDAY, APRIL 17, 1997

C1

FURNITURE '97

The Retro
And the Restless:
Two Milans

Experiments

ROSENTHAL

Droog Design

for Rosenthal

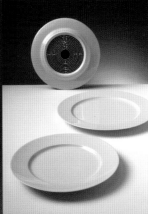

Microwave plate

Arnout Visser
1997
porcelain, iron oxide
glaze
Ø 31 x 2.5 cm

Eggshell vase

Marcel Wanders
1997
porcelain
9 x 9 x 10 cm

Foam bowl

Marcel Wanders
1997
porcelain
22 x 22 x 7 cm

DROOG DESIGN FOR ROSENTHAL

"EXPERIMENTS IN PORCELAIN"

An important meeting

The meeting between Rosenthal and Droog Design is a truly important event. One of the world's most important porcelain manufacturers, with an unrivalled tradition of research and innovation that has led to its cooperation with the greatest designers and artists of the twentieth Century, has teamed up with a group of young Dutch designers that, starting from its first official appearance in Milan during the 1993 Salone del Mobile, has revolutionised and influenced the entire world of design with their "dry" proposals (droog = dry). This project is a great opportunity for Droog Design, because it is their very first commission from an established company.

Experiments in porcelain

The project, whose idea first emerged in May 1996, aims to study the new expressive potential of porcelain applied to traditional objects and new product types. Gijs Bakker, Hella Jongerius, Marcel Wanders, Dick van Hoff and Arnout Visser have brought their own creativity and, at times, bizarre inspiration to Rosenthal's Design-Studio in Selb, where their ideas have been turned into reality. The result is a total of 12 objects with surprising shapes (Marcel Wanders' vases), decorations (Gijs Bakker's *knitted Maria*), type (Hella Jongerius' stool), functionality (Dick van Hoff's monocoque lamp), and materials (Arnout Visser's *magnetron* dishes).

The exhibit

A simple exhibit designed by Gijs Bakker and Marcel Wanders for the Rosenthal Studio-Haus of Milan will be displaying the prototypes during the 1997 Salone del Mobile (April 9 - 14). Afterwards, the collection will be shown in a travelling exhibit that will bring Droog Design all over the world and in several events organised by the leading Rosenthal Studio-Haus centres in Europe. The events will present the results of this work to a broader public and also be used to evaluate possible mass-production of the objects

archiefdoos "DD for Rosenthal project" / "P"

Rosenthal Italia s.r.l.
20134 Milano
via Raffaele Rubattino, 4
tel. 02/2152241 - Fax: 02/2153182

Porcelain stool

Hella Jongerius
1997
porcelain
50 x 40 x 25 cm

**Presentation Rosenthal,
Frankfurt Fair, February 14-18**

Sponge vase

Marcel Wanders
1997
porcelain
10 x 10 x 6 cm

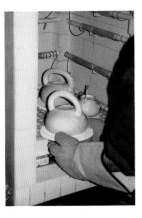

Droog Design

Januari 1997 1

quarterly newsletter

Droog Design Foundation
Keizersgracht 518 1017 EK Amsterdam
Telephone +31 20 638 29 86 Fax +31 20 638 88 28

Plastics new treat
presentation Milan '96

The 1996 Droog Design presentation at the Salone Del Mobile was visited by more people than ever before. On opening day the crowds were enormous and the police had to be called in to control the traffic outside the building.

The attention of the press was - again - overwhelming. In the August issue of the Italian magazine Domus there was an eight-page, richly illustrated article about Droog Design and the English Blueprint of October 1996 published a long interview with Droog Design entitled 'What is Droog?'. Central theme in this fourth edition of Droog Design was the re-assessment of plastics. Now that plastics have turned out to be less harmful to the environment than they were originally thought to be, their popularity is growing by the minute and their technical and aesthetical qualities are being improved.

Droog Design focused on the craft-slike approach of the material and a new application of existing techniques. A press release quote: 'Lightsources which are 'difficult' to implement like the old familiar TL tube and the PL lamp are 'wrapped' in inflatable pvc. Dick van Hoff stitched together pieces of felt, which he used as a basis for a washbasin which was then drenched in polyester resin. And Arian Brekveld breathed new life into old pvc dipping techniques. Implementation of a lamp lends the material a new transparent quality'.

Co-operation with Rosenthal

The Milan exhibition made, the German china manufacturer Rosenthal, contact Droog Design for an experimental project. After an introductory visit to the factory in Selb six designers, directed by Gijs Bakker, 'plunged' into the china. Since then several ideas have been developed which will be carried out by Rosenthal. Before working in Selb some designers have been executing their first experiments at the European Ceramic Work Centre in s' Hertogenbosch. In april '97 the results of the project will be presented in the Rosenthal showroom at Corso Mattiotti during the Salone del Mobile in Milan.

Dry Tech chair big hit in Milan

'This object was the true revelation of the entire Salone, the only object worth seeing,' Interni magazine commented in its assessment of the presentations at and round the Salone del Mobile, Milan 1996. This macramé chair was a design made by Marcel Wanders as part of Dry Tech, a project of Droog Design Foundation in co-operation with the Aviation and Space laboratory of Delft Technical University. (See information in another part of this newsletter). Marcel Wanders knotted a fabric of carbon and aramid fibres, which - dipped in epoxy - was hung at four corners, determining its shape. The chair has since been bought by the Eindhoven Academy of Industrial Design and the Museum of Modern Art in New York (from the Dry Tech project MOMA also bought Hella Jongerius' knitted lamp), the Textile Museum in Tilburg (which had already added Tejo Remy's rag chair to its collection before) and the Technology Museum in Delft.

Newsletter 1, January 1997
design Ontwerpwerk

Utrecht Central Museum Purchase

The Utrecht Central Museum purchases the entire Collection Droog Design 1993-1996 that now consists of 37 products. The museum organizes a large exhibition, accompanied by a book written by curator of design Ida van Zijl. It is designed by the Dutch graphic design studio Gonnissen and Widdershoven (now Thonik). It features special photography: the shooting has taken place at the home of the graphic designers themselves, all products are pictured in use.

010 publishers launches the book 'Droog Design. Spirit of the Nineties', edited by Renny Ramakers and Gijs Bakker. The book has been designed by Dutch graphic designer Roelof Mulder. Paola Antonelli, curator of design and architecture of the Museum of Modern Art has written the introduction.

Keine Diskussionen, keine demo-
kratischen Beschlüsse – Droog wird
absolutistisch regiert. Zwei Köpfe
entscheiden, was Trend sein soll: der
Designer Gijs Bakker, 55 Jahre, und
die Designkritikerin Renny Ramakers,
51 Jahre, hier unter „85 lamps".

DER DROOG-VIRUS GEHT UM

Bevorzugt findet man ihn an Orten, die der zeitlose Zeitgeist fest in den Fängen hat. In den Modetempeln von Giorgio Armani, im Paramount Hotel in New York, im MoMA oder auf den Seiten führender Designmagazine – überall begegnet man den Objekten der holländischen Gruppe Droog Design.

Auf der diesjährigen Möbelmesse in Mailand hat sie es wieder geschafft: Zum fünften Mal in Folge wurden ihre Neuheiten zum Straßengespräch der verwöhnten Besucherschar. Badfliesen mit integriertem Fernsehmonitor! Wasserhähne, die, je nach Wassertemperatur, rot oder blau leuchten! Die Talentschmiede aus Amsterdam war wieder in Hochform – wie schon bei ihrem ersten Mailänder Auftritt 1993. Da präsentierte Droog eine „Kommode", die aus scheinbar willkürlich übereinander gestapelten Schubladen bestand. Ein Band, das außen herumgewickelt war, bewahrte das Ganze davor, auseinanderzufallen. Vom selben Designer, Tejo Remy, stammt eine Lampe aus 12 von der Decke hängenden und mit Glühbirnen gefüllten Milchflaschen. Und Rody Graumans hatte 85 Glühbirnen gebündelt und die Stromkabel wie einen Pferdeschwanz zusammengebunden. Der Name des Kronleuchters von brachialem Baumarkt-Charme war so lakonisch wie das Design: „85 Lamps".

Nach diesem Urknall folgten Jahr für Jahr Kollektionen, die die Designwelt verstörten oder entzückten, aber auf keinen Fall gleichgültig ließen. In Holland genießt Droog inzwischen Kultstatus. Das MoMA in New York hat Droog-Objekte in kurzer Folge gleich für zwei Ausstellungen ausgewählt:

Text **Karl Armer** Fotos **Tom Nagy**

DROOG

Kühl, pfiffig und widerspruchsvoll ist das Design.

Architektur & Wohnung 4, 1997

...nter diesem Label aus Holland kommt und rund um die Welt Furore gemacht hat

Nicht große Designer, sondern
alle starken Frauen sind Vorbilder
von Hella Jongerius, 34 Jahre.
Droog wählte schon ihre Examens-
arbeit aus, eine Bademattte, und
auch alle nachfolgenden Entwürfe.
Die medienträchtige Promotion
hat positive Folgen, Cappellini und
Authentics winken mit Aufträgen.

HELLA JONGERIUS

Objekt: „Soft Vase", 1995
Material: Polyurethan

Auflage: Serie

Hersteller: DMD

Preis: 125 Mark

Vor allem die technischen und
physikalischen Möglichkeiten eines
Materials interessieren Arnout
Visser, 35 Jahre. Daß Glas in erhitztem
Zustand flüssig ist und dann wie
Wassertropfen zu Boden fällt, moti-
vierte ihn zum Entwurf dieser
Kacheln. Droog nahm sie sofort in
die aktuelle Badekollektion auf.

ARNOUT VISSER

Objekt: „Floortiles", 1997
Material: Keramik und Glas

Auflage: Prototyp

Hersteller: Koninklijk Mosa

Entwicklungspreis: 250 Mark pro qm

Trotz aller Suche hat sich noch
keine Firma gefunden, die Dick van
Hoffs Wasserhahn herstellen will.
Zu unprätentiös wirkt das Objekt des
Achille-Castiglioni-Fans, 26 Jahre.
Gerade das gefiel den Geschmacks-
päpsten von Droog, sie zeigten
das Werk des frisch von der Schul-
bank Kommenden in Mailand.

DICK
VAN HOFF

Objekt: „Stop-Tap", 1995

Material: Kupferrohr, Standardgewinde

Auflage: limitiert auf 20 Stück

Hersteller: Dick van Hoff

Preis: 750 Gulden

RICHARD HUTTEN

OLANDA
ELOGIO DELLA FOLLIA

Holland: in Praise of Folly

Dal paese più civilizzato d'Europa, tre diverse lezioni di design su come convivere con il degrado materiale e culturale dell'epoca industriale: l'esistenzialismo di Droog, l'utopia alternativa degli squatters, il neomodernismo applicato al recupero di un edificio ■ From Europe's most civilised country, three very different design lessons on how to live with the physical and cultural dereliction of the industrial age: Droog existentialism, a squatters' alternative utopia, and neo-modernism applied to building renovation

A CASA CON DROOG

Persone, luoghi e oggetti d'affezione dietro Droog Design, oltre la cortina mediatica che ne fa il simbolo del nuovo radical-chic ■ Backstage at Droog Design: the people, places and objects behind the media curtain that has made the studio a symbol of the new radical-chic

STEFANO CASCIANI. Amsterdam – o meglio quella straordinaria conurbazione che è oggi l'Olanda – sarebbe una buona capitale per l'Europa che ci aspetta nel Terzo millennio. Poco a che fare con gli sconquassi millenari di Roma, con il triste passato di Bruxelles (massacri urbanistici e non), con Parigi "qui a perdu son âme", Londra in trance da boom, Berlino non ancora pronta... Le persone, i luoghi e perfino le cose incontrate in questo viaggio in Olanda hanno l'aria di riuscire in qualche modo a comporre il conflitto culturale permanente tra ieri, oggi e domani. Disperati come tutti gli europei, ma forse un po' più colti, gli olan-

→

● **A destra:** Richard Hutten, panca "The Cross", 1994.
Nella pagina a lato: Gijs Bakker (Amersfoort, 1942), fondatore con Renny Remakers, di Droog Design, con il tavolo "Fruitbake with Holes" 1993

a cura di/edited by Stefano Casciani

foto Jacek P. Sołtan

At home with Droog. *Amsterdam, or rather the amazing conurbation that is the Netherlands today, would make a good capital for the Europe that awaits us in the Third Millennium – little of Rome's millennia-old muddle, none of Brussels' unhappy past (massacres and otherwise), and quite unlike Paris "qui a perdu son âme", London mesmerised economic and cultural boom, or Berlin which still isn't ready yet. The people, places and even objects I saw on this trip to the Netherlands seemed, in one way or another, to be making a success of resolving the eternal cultural conflict between past, present and future. Despairing like all Europeans,*

● **Left:** Richard Hutten, "The Cross", bench seat, 1994.
Opposite page: Gijs Bakker (Amersfoort, 1942), co-founder with Renny Remakers of Droog Design.

tto: Marcel Wanders,
un prototipo di lampada
ssuto, 1997. **Nella pagina**
to: Johannes Vermeer,
ettera d'amore (particolare),
9-1670, Rijksmuseum,
sterdam.
llow: Marcel Wanders
a fabric lamp prototype, 1997
osite: Johannes
meer, The Love-Letter (detail),
9-1670, Rijksmuseum,
sterdam.

desi non sembrano darsi troppa pena delle angosce futuribili ("Non gli interessa quel che c'è stato prima", dice John Tackara, direttore del nuovo, brillante Dutch Design Institute), si muovono nel presente con atti decisi, provocatori, rispettosi soprattutto degli insegnamenti di Erasmo da Rotterdam: esprimono una follia lucida, coltivata, contemporanea, cioè davvero progettuale nell'accogliere

ortodossi che ha rilanciato l'immagine un po' appannata del design olandese con il fenomeno Droog; parola-esorcismo, dal significato semplice: "secco" o meglio "asciutto", come il fisico di una persona, come una risposta precisa e diretta, uno statement deciso e definitivo, che non lascia spazio a repliche incerte. Droog si accetta o si rifiuta, è conscio della sua intenzione polemica. Si può

though perhaps ally aware, the disinclined to much about w may bring ("T terested in wh fore," observes director of the Dutch Design adopt a brisk attitude to the all, they hav mus of Rotte ings very much folly is crisp, contemporary, ly design-ori way it deals things, which cepted or mov ways, in tru fashion, with final judgeme sooner or later actual achieve than good inte. This may expl ly-mounting s small thoug group of unort garde Droog have revived L somewhat tarr exorcism, the simply means haps more accu as word of a p or "crisp" as rect, precise an tion – a decis tive statement room for unce sponse. Droog of its own poli which you eit reject: there ar sures Could an insincerely to made of rubbe gerius) or fel Hoff, or vase baked sponge kaolin (Marce These objects posed to hum friendly adve dustrial desig day: their aim a behavioural psychological (i they demand be

Sotto: Dick van Hoff (Arnhem, 1970) nella soffitta-studio-abitazione
n il prototipo di un orologio di cemento, da lui-stesso realizzato
ampo compreso). **Nella pagina a lato:** Hella Jongerius (Rotterdam
963) nel bagno del suo studio, con il lavabo "Washbowl" e il "soapom
bagno di poliuretano morbido prodotto da DMD per Droog.

il dato esistente: nello stravolgerlo o nell'accettarlo, secondo l'ispirazione del momento, ma comunque – in ossequio alla regola protestante – in vista di un giudizio che prima o poi verrà, e sarà sulle opere compiute, non sulle intenzioni enunciate.
Dev'essere così che si è fatta lentamente strada quella piccola ma agguerrita avan

reagire retoricamente a un lavabo di gomma (Hella Jongerius) o di feltro (Dick van Hoff), a dei vasi ricavati dalla cottura di spugne imbevute di caolino (Marcel Wanders)? Davvero non sembra possibile. Questi oggetti non vogliono essere amabili, accattivanti, userfriendly, come la maggior parte della produzione proposta dall'immaginario in

thing Droog produces. I can't deny the fundamentally artistic intent of their objects: Man Ray's objects of affection and Marcel Duchamp's ready-mades are the direct antecedents of these lamps, vases, porcelain, furniture and other objects that draw intelligently on the Arts and Crafts tradition, rather than Bauhaus constructivist assemblage or the graceful elegance of Italian bel design. They seem intended for visual consumption, not mass production, on the part of a sophisticated public well versed in the expressive subtleties of a language whose rough-hewn "wildness" is apparent rather than real. Droog icons draw on a century of artistic and entrepreneurial endeavour that has seen real things as possible raw material for philosophical and (why not?) commercial discourse. This particular kind of object-animism sublimated in the attitudes of designers – those portrayed here – who seek to identify the vital essence, the capacity to elicit love, hate or indifference, in the physical things they make (some, admittedly, are most unlikely to have any practical use in the real world). Excepting the founding father Gijs Bakker, the Droog designers I met – most were youthful and some were very young – lived in microscopic rooms (often at the top of incredibly steep staircases with step-riser ratios seemingly tailor-made to the giant strides of an anomalous superraces, temporary lodgings or makeshift workshops. All of them appeared about to move from their present workshops to some new studio or a house under construction in Amsterdam, Rotterdam or Arnhem, the apices of an animated urban triangle which the designers choose to live in as the mood of the moment takes them. As a result, their objects seem the only anchors they have in everyday reality, signs marking their passage across the face of the earth, evidence that, long ago, they too once considered living in houses before moving on yet again from one temporary dwelling to another.
This may be why the link with physical matter – the quintessential alchemy of contemporary design distorted and overwhelmed by eagerness for change and interpretation, the need to communicate rather than shape – seems so important in these people and things. Thus, Droog forms are:
- archetypal (Dick van Hoff's taps and table clock);
- geometrical and primary (Gijs Bakker's parallelepiped – though perforated – furniture; Richard Hutten's crossshaped table sofas);
- organic and natural (Marcel Wanders' porcelain sponges and eggs, and aramid-fibre mesh chairs);
- uniformed (Hella Jongerius' vases and rubber washbasins). In other words, Droog forms are non-forms, borrowed from other permanently existing worlds, that have temporarily been bent to a radical artistic purpose. There's nothing chic, affected or artificial about these people, their products and their homes, just an embarrassing sincerity, a shameless insistence that designers are ordinary people working for (or against) industry armed only with ideas and manual skills, people who have no need of limousines, bijou attic apartments (in town) or chalets (in the mountains).
S.C.

a **Above:** Dick van Hoff (Arnhem, 1970) in his attic studio dwelling
with the prototype of a concrete clock made entirely by himself
(including the mould). **Opposite page:** Hella Jongerius (Rotterdam

MARCEL WANDERS

MARCEL WANDERS

DICK VAN HOFF

1998

Presentation Milan, April 16-21

The Inevitable Ornament

Gijs Bakker, Niels van Eijk, Rody Graumans,
Djoke de Jong, Hella Jongerius, Dick van Hoff,
Peter Hopman, Richard Hutten, Matijs
Korpershoek, Erik Jan Kwakkel, Jan Melis,
Saar Oosterhof, Tejo Remy, Frank Tjepkema,
Arnout Visser, Marcel Wanders

Mirror image Droog Design invites MVRDV
Architects to design an installation for the
presentation of 'The Inevitable Ornament'.
MVRDV comes up with the idea to cover the
whole space with a woven screen decorated
with a panoramic picture of a traffic junction
in Rotterdam. The design is beautiful, but unfortunately during the process of fixing the screen
to ceilings and walls, it turns out that the picture
is printed in its mirror image and can not be
used. The day before the opening the Droog
Design team is forced to develop a totally new
concept and to pillage the city of Milan for the
needed materials. The installation, consisting
of an extremely long table through the entire
space is ready just in time and the visitors are
in awe, again.

The Inevitable Ornament

Droog Design likes to change perspectives.
Always being associated with simplicity,
Droog sets up a project called 'The Inevitable
Ornament', to express the fact that their basic
approach can well coincide with decoration.
In their case, however, it is not merely skin
deep, not an extra, but it evolves from the
concept in a logical, natural way.
'The Inevitable Ornament' is presented in
Spazio Solferino in Milan, showing well known
products like the '85 lamps' chandelier and a
number of new ones. Among them is the misty
mirror by Matijs Korpershoek. This mirror has
been covered with an invisible coating in such
a way that decoration or text appears just by
breathing on it.
Unfortunately the people who have been
charged to clean the exhibition space are so
thorough that they also clean the mirror and
consequently kill it.

Misty mirror

Matijs Korpershoek
1998
mirror, treated with chemicals
57 x 39.5 cm

Domus, January 1998

Testo di *Text by* Renny Ramakers

Droog Design

Un nuovo tipo di consumatore
Cultura speculare significa ribaltare la prospettiva corrente. Non basta essere alternativi per sfuggire al meccanismo di mercato. Secondo la teorica e co-fondatrice del gruppo olandese, al design oggi serve una vera riflessione sui contenuti, svincolata dalla richieste della società.

A new type of consumer
Mirrored culture means the reversal of today's perspective. It is not enough to be alternative to escape the market mechanism. According to the theorist and co-founder of the Dutch group, design today needs genuine reflection on contents, disengaged from the demands of society.

La nostra cultura si fa sempre più variegata e le tendenze mutano a una velocità spaventosa. Gli stili si accavallano; nei negozi c'è soltanto l'imbarazzo della scelta, che si tratti di seggiole da cucina o di cavatappi, si trovano oggetti per tutti i gusti e all'orizzonte si staglia la prospettiva ammiccante della produzione di massa personalizzata. 'Customisation' è la formula magica che avvicina ogni cliente al proprio prodotto. Nell'industria automobilistica e del ciclo sono già disponibili prodotti su misura, e le possibilità offerte da Internet rendono la formula ancor più realizzabile. Si specificano i requisiti desiderati standosene comodamente seduti in poltrona e il lavoro è presto fatto. Miracoli dell'era postindustriale! Grazie al computer si torna alla produzione di pezzi singoli, ma solo così la nostra cultura si trasforma.

Tuttavia l'apparenza inganna. Certamente non esistono due esemplari uguali nell'esercito di aspirapolvere esposti nei negozi, e le differenze balzano agli occhi. È evidente comunque che ci si sforza di rendere ogni aspirapolvere il più possibile simile agli altri, e persino a prodotti di diverso tipo, tanto che chi vuole comprare un ferro da stiro a volte pensa di essere finito in un negozio di scarpe sportive. La nostra cultura in effetti è estremamente varia, ma la varietà si compone di elementi molto simili fra loro. La differenziazione si ottiene attraverso modificazioni minime nella forma; i prodotti vengono adattati alle diverse culture e ai relativi gusti, mentre le eventuali diversità funzionali vengono spazzate via. Anche i cosiddetti prodotti su misura partono da uno schema fisso: di certo non si può ancora ordinare un'auto rettangolare. Il modello della 'customisation' non si basa sulla produzione personalizzata ma sulla produzione standard personalizzata, il che porta a chiedersi se il consumatore possa o voglia pensare a qualcosa di diverso.

La cultura dell'immagine soffre praticamente del medesimo male. I media ci bombardano quotidianamente di immagini sempre nuove, che però raramente o mai arrivano in profondità. Tutto si svolge con grande rapidità e segue quasi sempre la stessa ricetta, tanto che le immagini si rovesciano addosso allo spettatore in una sorta di poltiglia informe.

Nella cultura attuale la varietà è soltanto apparente; in realtà ci stiamo avviando verso una sorta di monocultura, dominata da una singola ideologia, che è quella di guadagnare il massimo nel più breve tempo possibile. Gli esperti di marketing decidono cosa si deve produrre; i progettisti fanno la parte del leone nel campo dell'edilizia; l'architettura è diventata un bene di consumo e la maggioranza degli architetti si adegua alla situazione. Gli studi di progettazione sono stati assorbiti completamente nel sistema industriale e si sono trasformati in imprese al servizio del cliente. Quasi mai si può parlare di novità fondamentali nella produzione, e chi ha il coraggio di investire in progetti innovativi viene subito copiato. Il design è diventato uno stile, un mezzo per incrementare le vendite, un'operazione

commerciale. Persino le subculture vengono sfruttate a livello industriale. Grandi compagnie come la Nike e la Coca Cola cercano di raggiungere una "street credibility" servendosi di progettisti che vengono dall'"underground" "Underground goes mainstream" era il titolo chiarificatore di una conferenza tenutasi in novembre ad Amsterdam. Ogni cultura implica una controcultura, ma parte di questa viene immediatamente assorbita, almeno temporaneamente, nella cosiddetta mainstream (cultura dominante) e accetta di buon grado questo processo. In questo periodo di transizione, essere 'alternativi' è fatica sprecata. Il denaro è potere e il successo è tale soltanto se implica alti guadagni.

A mano a mano che la mainstream prende piede, chi mantiene la propria autonomia e va controcorrente viene sospinto ai margini. Gli 'emarginati' destano grande interesse, perché vivacizzano l'ambiente e fanno sensazione, ma niente di più, anche perché in fin dei conti l'interesse assomiglia più che altro a una sorta di tolleranza repressiva.

Il treno si allontana sferragliando. Di tanto in tanto bisogna rallentare o scegliere un altro binario, ma subito dopo la velocità viene triplicata. I cambiamenti che avvengono sotto le pressioni sociali non superano i confini di ciò che viene considerato economicamente accettabile. Dal punto di vista sociologico, l'ideale sarebbe una società durevole; invece non facciamo che produrre e consumare sempre di più. La cultura viene determinata dal mercato. Si produce ciò che si vende, e questo significa che siamo in balia della dispersività. La chirurgia estetica è estremamente diffusa, e chiunque può modificare il proprio corpo a seconda dei propri desideri, ma sembra che tutti perseguano il medesimo ideale di bellezza. Presto il brutto e il vecchio non esisteranno più; qualsiasi diversità verrà appianata. Andiamo incontro alla dittatura della mediocrità, a un livellamento culturale generale.

Nel suo libro *Winners! How Today's Successful Companies Innovate by Design* (Amsterdam, 1997), John Thackara si dimostra ottimista nei confronti dei consumatori del futuro. Prendendo spunto dall'invecchiamento della società, afferma che i consumatori diventeranno più saggi con l'età. "I consumatori diventano più anziani e più consapevoli dei problemi ambientali con il risultato che qualità, durata e rapporto qualità/prezzo hanno più peso nelle scelte che non i prodotti sgargianti e dalla vita breve o i beni di marche famose". Ma gli uomini di oggi, che fra qualche tempo diventeranno più vecchi e più saggi, per il momento consumano in abbondanza; sorge quindi il dubbio legittimo che il loro comportamento possa modificarsi realmente. E poi, perché mai a ottant'anni si dovrebbe acquistare un prodotto destinato a durarne altri trenta? Quello della "terza età" è diventato in ogni caso un pubblico ambito che gli esperti di marketing sanno bene come sfruttare.

Ha più senso la visione del futuro descritta recentemente dal progettista britannico Ross Lovegrove in occasione di una conferenza sul design tenuta in Finlandia: "La forza

motrice del futuro sarà il consumismo spinto al parossismo dai produttori". Che gli aspetti economici siano diventati dominanti nella nostra cultura è un dato di fatto, e su questo non si può tornare indietro. Resta da chiedersi se lo vorremmo davvero; personalmente penso di no. Tutti siamo grandi consumatori e la moderazione finisce per diventare un anacronismo. "Ogni epoca anela a un mondo migliore", scrisse lo storico olandese Johan Huizinga nel suo libro *L'autunno del Medioevo*, pubblicato nel 1919. La nostra non fa eccezione, ma attualmente pensiamo che il solo modo per ottenere un mondo migliore sia quello di produrre il più possibile. Il problema della durevolezza è senz'altro scottante, anche nel campo dell'architettura e del design. Come si potrebbe evitare che in futuro si continui a gettare via gli oggetti troppo rapidamente? In una pubblicazione apparsa di recente, intitolata *Eternally Yours, Visions on Product Endurance* (Rotterdam, 1997), vengono elencate numerose proposte. L'una auspica la trasformazione dei prodotti in servizi, l'altra vede la salvezza nei prodotti cosiddetti "morali". Per quanto possa essere utile porsi il problema della durevolezza, tuttavia, si potrà ottenere qualche risultato soltanto se tutti si impegneranno a operare in questa direzione. A questo proposito mi viene in mente l'efficace risposta data da Ettore Sottsass (*Domus*, settembre 1997) a chi gli chiedeva che cosa significassero per lui termini come 'ecologia' e 'sostenibilità': "Deve preoccuparsi dell'ecologia chi fa le navi da guerra e usa tonnellate d'acciaio. Non lo vengano a dire a me che faccio una maniglia ogni cinque anni".

Per quanto possiamo girare attorno al discorso, dobbiamo ammettere che ormai siamo incatenati al sistema, con tutti i suoi vantaggi e svantaggi; quindi non rimane altro da fare che sviluppare un sistema parallelo, una cultura speculare che ristabilisca l'equilibrio. Tale cultura, che è precisamente il contrario della mainstream sotto tutti i punti di vista, presta attenzione alle questioni che ora nella fretta vengono trascurate, agli aspetti non immediati e magari un po' spiacevoli. Non essendo rivolta unicamente al guadagno, privilegia i valori morali, però non si pone nemmeno la modificazione della mainstream come missione da compiere. L'unica missione è quella di essere se stessi, e la mainstream d'altronde si appropria di tutto ciò che è di suo gusto. A questo punto è il caso di porsi una domanda fondamentale, cioè se la cultura sia favorita dal fatto che espressioni autonome esercitino il loro influsso sulla produzione di massa, anche sé tale influsso sarà sempre superficiale. Gli elementi salienti di Memphis venivano da una ridotta avanguardia attiva nel campo e furono elaborati in seguito, ma la produzione di massa, che attira gran parte dei designer nella propria scia, ha assorbito soltanto le caratteristiche esterne. Anche per questo motivo il design è diventato uno stile, ma si tratta di un fenomeno che non deve necessariamente renderci felici. Invece di tanti surrogati annacquati dell'originale che creano l'immagine quotidiana, sarebbe meglio che

Daedalus Prize Droog Design wins the first edition of the Daedalus Prize of European Design 'for its extraordinary originality and cultural, organizational and methodological skills'. The jury, Alessandro Mendini, Andrea Branzi, Gilda Bojardi and Francois Burckhardt, has also nominated Konstantin Grcic, Alfredo Häberli, Ferrucio Lavani and Ilkka Suppanen.

Dry Bathing revisited

An installation of the now two year old project Dry Bathing is purchased by the French Fonds National d'Art Contemporain. Dry Bathing has a terrific presentation at Moss in New York.

Organic design: Matt Schwab's
lettuce lamp was a hit with
Droog's Renny Ramakers.

OBJET, EVERYDAY

Sydney Design Week '98 was an unqualified success, celebrating design
for the people, by the people. DUGALD JELLIE reports.

Droog addicts: Andreas Möller's
Botle-Box for tulips (above), a novel
approach to Holland's excess manur
problem, and Marcel Wanders's
Eggshell Vase (below), moulded
from an egg-stuffed condom.

SMH August 20, 199

Domain, the Sydney Morning Herald, your Life and Home Weekly, July 30, 1998

DROOG ADDICTION

With Sydney Design Week almost upon us,
ANTONIA WILLIAMS talks to the star turn.

Domain, the Sydney Morning Herald, your Life and Home Weekly, July 30, 1998

DROOG ADDICTION

With Sydney Design Week almost upon us,
ANTONIA WILLIAMS talks to the star turn.

OBJE Ϯ, ΕV

Sydney Design Week '98 was an unqualifi
for the people, by the people. DU

Sydney Design Week Renny Ramakers is special guest at Sydney Design Week. She gives a lecture at the Powerhouse museum and a five day workshop at the College of Fine Arts. Instead of diving into the design process right away, she urges the students to determine the status of their own living environment and start from there. According to student Matt Schwab, Europe's leading edge design only reaches him through publications. To him the mere experience of a product's image is sufficient. He reasons that design itself can have built-in-temporariness and by wrapping a lettuce leaf around a light bulb he makes a lamp that only lasts a few minutes, just to take a look. He is not very happy that pictures are made of his lamp but when it is published in Droog's newsletter, he writes a letter to ask for a copy, although he has to admit: 'By asking for a newsletter I think I cheat a little bit…'.

YDNEY Design Week started as the celebration of everyday objects. It ended last weekend with, perhaps, a new spin: the democracy of design. Design for everyone.

This was the theme underlying so many of the lectures, exhibitions, workshops – even the shopping sprees – that made up Design Week '98. Design is for the people. Design is about people. Design is about the ideas of everyone.

The upshot? It was a week in which design took centre stage, with sell-out lectures and brisk trading at all design-savvy inner-city furniture showrooms.

eggs? A tulip bulb box made from, well, cow turds? A plastic artificial plant?

As Ramakers said during her keynote lecture at the Powerhouse Museum: "With design, everything is possible."

But back to the democracy of design. This theme received a holistic embrace on Monday evening when James Weirick, professor of landscape architecture at the University of NSW, spoke about American architects Walter Burley Griffin and Marion Mahony.

Despite audio-visual hiccups, it was a lecture of scholarly rigour and intellectual insights that stimulated and aroused the audience of mainly archi-

She spoke growing up furnishings recent wor motherhood display, aga

Her le approach – impressive tures works internationa

Followin was Renny tle introduc with images that often u design upsi

It was th

Dessert On behalf of Droog Design, Gijs Bakker is leading a project 'Dessert' for Alessi, with three selected students from the Institute for System and Product Design in Bremerhafen. Research is done into dessert habits in various cultures. The results are presented in an installation in the swimming pool of the institute. Alberto Alessi chooses the ice bowl by Sebastian Liedtke as best product.

dutch f

Holland Herald (KLM) January 1998

Dutch
on display

The Droog Design Foundation promotes the cream of home-grown creativity. *Christine Aziz* meets its founders and looks at some classic prototypes. Portrait by *Albert Roosenburg*

Five years ago, designers Gijs Bakker and Renny Ramakers took a collection of work by young Dutch designers to the world's most important design showcase, the International Furniture Fair in Milan. The collection caused quite a stir and word got around that this was THE collection to see. Encouraged, Bakker and Ramakers returned to set up the Droog Design Foundation, a non-profit making company which selects and promotes the best of Dutch design. It not only established The Netherlands as a source of creative and innovative young designers but gave birth to a movement that has become a major influence on Nineties design.

But what is Droog (the word for 'dry' in Dutch, and pronounced drogue)? According to Bakker, Droog style incorporates the national traits of his homeland: "It's self-effacing, ironic and simple. After all the visual violence of Eighties post-modernism there was a need for going back to basics and simplicity. The Dutch could fill this gap with their spirit and irony."

Every year the foundation selects design prototypes by young Dutch designers for international promotion and possible production. Each item has to

reflect the Droog philosophy. "We have to look at concept, the idea behind the product," says Bak "We have to ask whether it says anything. How d it deal with the material? Does it say anything nev about production and its function?"

Very often, items promoted by Droog are visu puns. "It's all about material, not form," says Droo fan Murray Moss, owner of Moss design store in York's chic SoHo. They take something simple, li plain white tile and make a big deal out of it. That just a prototype isn't the point. The point is that e one who looks at it goes, 'Ah!'."

Bakker's own design roots lie in jewelery. He trained at the Instituut voor Kunstnijverheid Onder in Amsterdam (now known as the Gerrit Rietveld Academy) between 1958 and 1963, and is now a partment head at the Design Academy in Eindhov His exploitation of unusual materials (for example, aluminium stovepipe for a necklace), is reflected widely throughout Droog Design. The foundation encourages its designers to experiment with new materials and technology. Four designers worked the aviation and space laboratory at Technische Universiteit Delft (Delft Technical University) to pro duce designs that displayed an adventurous mix o

Opposite:
Ramakers and Bakker felt a need for going back to basics.
Top, right: Andreas Möller's 'Dutch souvenir'.
Above: Marcel Wanders' 'sponge' vase made for Rosenthal

new
items
for the
home

They have worked with the likes of Mandarin Duck, Cappellini, Flos and Cacharel. They are revered by the design world internationally and held up as the darlings of the avant-garde. Yet, *who* or *what* is Amsterdam-based Droog Design? Here we present five years of Droog production and attempt to unravel the Droog 'phenomenon', while, from the north, Stephen Todd finds them a place within the context of Dutch tradition.

Designers' Workshop, October 1998

1999

Presentation Milan, April 13-18

Couleur Locale, Droog Design for Oranienbaum
Jurgen Bey, Martí Guixé, Hella Jongerius, Traast
& Gruson, Marcel Wanders
+
A Touch of Glass, Droog Design for Salviati
Matijs Korpershoek, Marcel Wanders
+
Play House, Droog Design for Bang & Olufsen
Traast & Gruson

The results of the project 'Couleur Locale,
Droog Design for Oranienbaum' are first
shown in Milan. A few months later the project
is presented in Oranienbaum. That also means
the end of the project. A few local companies
show interest but their financial situation does
not allow them to invest in production and
distribution. Attempts to interest local cultural
and commercial organisations to support the
project fail.

Couleur Locale, Droog Design for Oranienbaum The project 'Couleur Locale, Droog Design for Oranienbaum' highlights regional design. Oranienbaum is a little town south-west of Berlin in the former Eastern part of Germany. The castle of Oranienbaum, surrounded by a big landscape garden, was built by a Dutch princess of Oranje Nassau in the 17th century. Eager to preserve this Dutch-German cultural heritage for future generations, the Dutch government decided in 1997 to contribute to its restoration. This is based on a concept delivered by the local Cultural Foundation Dessau Wörlitz that is focusing on restoration, revival and innovation. For the latter two this foundation asks Droog Design to develop concepts. After a visit to Oranienbaum Droog Design comes up with the idea to design a number of products which fit in whatever the region has to offer and eventually should be produced there to revive economic activity, attract more tourists and add 'joie de vivre' to the region.
They aim to add a new cultural dimension in a way that both respects the soul of the area and gives it a contemporary interpretation. The key notions are: tradition, history and innovation, art and culture, nature and ecology, education and recreation, the relationship with the Netherlands, trade and economy and employment.
Droog Design asks Hella Jongerius, Marcel Wanders, Jurgen Bey and Martí Guixé, the first foreign designer to join Droog, to unleash Droog's mentality on regional conditions. The designers combine utility and beauty in new concepts for local materials and products and suggest ways to enjoy the impressive gardens. The project results in a large number of concepts.

Local traditional specialities have been the inspiration for Martí Guixé. The round base of his orange liqueur glass is faceted on the sides, which results in four different measures of drink depending on the position in which you lay down the glass on the table. The double wall of his earthenware flower vase contains real Oranienbaum soil. Guixé also designs a portable wooden orange peeler and a natural smell tester for tourists to take home the natural smell of Oranienbaum. His Oranienbaum candy contains an orange seed and a poplar wooden stick. One eats the candy, plants the seed and puts the stick next to it as a warning that in 20 years' time there will be an orange tree.

Martí Guixé:
'In Oranienbaum I noticed the boredom and the stillness of nature. And the peace that makes me nervous. A nature made only for looking, a big park where you can not interact, like a big scenario. An out of time, artificial vision of nature.'

Natural Smell Tester

Martí Guixé
1999
poplar wood
15 x 4 x 0,3 cm

Orange liqueur glass

Martí Guixé
1999
glass
Ø 10 x 14 cm

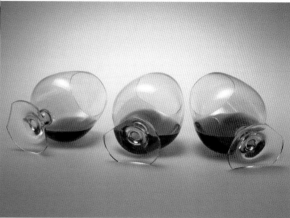

Earth flower vase

Martí Guixé
1999
glass, earth
11 x 16 x 25 cm

Sketch for 'earth flower vase'
Martí Guixé

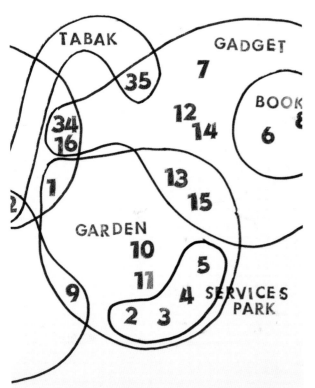

#32 HiT T

CONVENTIONAL   UNCONVENTIONAL

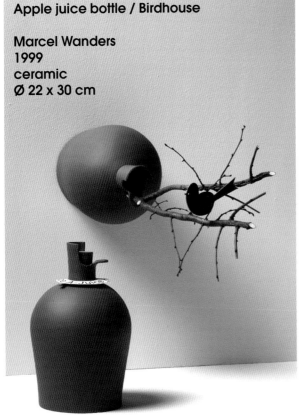

Apple juice bottle / Birdhouse

Marcel Wanders
1999
ceramic
Ø 22 x 30 cm

Marcel Wanders'
apple juice bottle-
birdhouse contains
the local apple juice.
When empty the bottle
can serve as a nesting
box for the many birds
in the region.

Marcel Wanders:
'I have focused on products that might contribute to the special character and atmosphere
the region has for the interested visitor, not just
because this makes the region even more
attractive, but also since this region has very
special qualities that might be unique and
important to the rest of the world.'

Marcel Wanders
2000
recycled plastic,
porcelain plate
30 x 30 x 15 cm

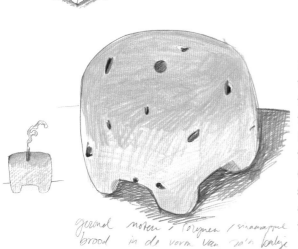

Sinaasappel
boompje

gerond noten / Torijnen / sinaasappel
brood in de vorm van zo'n boletje

Inspired by the orange tree in the typical
wooden container, Marcel Wanders designs
the Oranienbaumer Viereck, a new speciality
for the local bakers: each baker is supposed to
bake his own bread in the special tin. In addition
the Oranienbaumer biscuits are wrapped in a
cardboard box in the same wooden container
shape. When the biscuits are finished, the box
can be filled with compost and seeds to function as a greenhouse.

For active recreation
Wanders makes a
swing.

Willow chair

Marcel Wanders
1999
unpeeled willow shoot
Ø 80 x 78 cm

Disposable cutlery
and bowl

Marcel Wanders
1999
poplar wood
Ø 12 x 4 cm

To stimulate the local economy Marcel Wanders designs cutlery and bowls made of poplar wood and a willow chair to be produced by local craftsmen.

Packaging label

Hella Jongerius
1999
paper
4 x 10 cm

Packaging paper

Hella Jongerius
1999
paper
88 x 82 cm

Hella Jongerius:

'What struck me most was that spirits were so low in Oranienbaum and the surrounding area. The whole place was covered in a grey blanket. I was given a very simple mission: restore laughter.'

Among the designs of Hella Jongerius are a picnic mat with seats, packaging paper and labels for the local firms.

Picknick seats

Hella Jongerius
1999
wickerwork
40 x 20 x 14 cm

Picknick cloth

Hella Jongerius
1999
hemp
150 x 185 cm

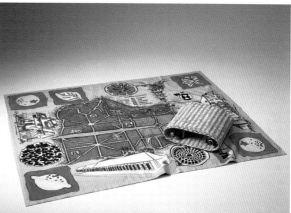

Jurgen Bey:

'Oranienbaum is a cultivated landscape in which nature and culture meet and influence each other, a protected area where the portraits of the eras have been frozen, and almost forgotten stories can survive. It is where souvenirs from all parts of the world have found a new place to stay and where guests have left their marks. The nice thing about these kinds of places is that they are a sort of collection of curiosities, a colourful mixture of objects that all tell their own story.'

For the park of Oranienbaum Jurgen Bey designs the tree trunk bench, a fallen tree in which bronze cast historical chair backs have been stuck, and a machine to extrude a gardening bench from park waste, such as hay, leaves and tree bark. It looks different every season.

Ornaments

The history of the estate and its residents is told by the ornaments. Silhouettes, family trees, maps and the like are cast in metal and turned into classic cast-iron garden benches with a modern look.

Ornamente

Die Geschichte des Landgutes und seiner Bewohner wird in Ornamenten erzählt. Silhouetten, Stammbäume, Grundrisse und dergleichen mehr werden in Metall gegossen und formen so klassische gußeiserne Parkbänke mit zeitgenössischer Ausstrahlung.

Couleur
Locale
Droog Design for/für Oranienbaum

The complete project is published in the booklet 'Couleur Locale' designed by Studio Gonnissen en Widdershoven (now Thonik) and contains the Audio CD 'Orange'.
Together with Ton Driessens, Marcel Wanders composes music based on all the basic sounds in the Oranienbaum area, such as the ones produced by swans, Trabant car doors banging, raindrops, children in the local school and much other everyday noise.

A Touch of Glass, Droog Design for Salviati

The Venetian company Salviati commissions Droog Design to create new artisan glass objects. Designers involved are Matijs Korpershoek, Erik Jan Kwakkel, Arnout Visser and Marcel Wanders. In addition, new ways to shape glass are explored, as well as principles for decoration. Droog Design shows the first results at the International Furniture Fair in Milan and Salviati takes one of Marcel Wanders' designs into production.

Graniglia

Marcel Wanders
1999
glass
Ø 43 x 10 cm

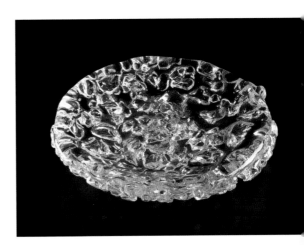

The Observer Magazine, July 11, 1999

Life**interiors**

The future's Orange

Can a band of hip Dutch designers revive one of Germany's dullest regions, in the heart of its former coal-mining belt? *By Ian Phillips*

In Dutch, the word 'droog' means dry. For many in the design world, however, it signifies everything that is hip, fashionable and funky. For those in the know, Droog is also a cooperative of designers set up in Amsterdam in 1992 with the aim of creating objects that display little ornamentation but a certain amount of 'dry' humour. Among the 60 items in their collection are a chair made out of old rags, a porcelain vase whose form was created by stuffing a condom full of eggs, and tables made from Swiss lace. One of their greatest fans is Karl Lagerfeld. 'Droog is the spirit of modernity,' he says. 'It is non-design and unpretentious.'

The region of Dessau-Wörlitz, in former East Germany, on the other hand, is anything but hip and happening. It used to be a coal-producing area until its mines were closed down in 1990. Nowadays, it has an unenviable unemployment rate of 25 per cent, and the words most often used to describe it are 'dull' and 'grey'.

At first sight, Droog and Dessau-Wörlitz seem to have absolutely nothing in common. But look further and you find that there is a link – a historic Dutch link. In 1659, Prince Georg of Anhalt-Dessau married Princess Henriette-Catherine of the House of Orange. 'She was very inspired by her home country,' says Dr Thomas Weiss of the local cultural organisation, the Kulturstiftung. 'For example, she built dykes to protect the landscape from the water of the River Elbe.' She also commissioned Dutch architect Cornelis Ryckwaert to build her a castle, which she named Oranienbaum.

In 1997, the Kulturstiftung received one million guilders (£300,000) from the Dutch government to restore the castle. It decided to devote some of the money to innovation, and commissioned Droog to create a series of objects inspired by the region. The results are on display until 5 September at the region's Third International Garden Festival.

Four designers were chosen to work on the project – three of them Dutch (Jurgen Bey, Hella Jongerius and Marcel Wanders) and one Spanish (Marti Guixé). 'The target was to create a revival in the region through design,' says one of Droog's co-founders, Renny Ramakers. 'We looked for companies in the area with which we could work. But there were hardly any.' The only one they found was a wickerwork factory, which has produced a basket chair for them.

Instead, the designers took their inspiration from traditional industries. In the castle park, for example, there is one of the largest orangeries in Europe, where

> **One of their biggest fans is Karl Lagerfeld. 'Droog is the spirit of modernity,' he declares. 'It is non-design and unpretentious'**

Clockwise, from top left: garden chairs; disposable cutlery and plate made with duplex press. Below, Oranienbaum castle

Ramakers describes it as a new way of looking at souvenirs. 'Instead of taking home a piece of pottery from the region, you take home a smell,' she declares.

'We saw that in the park, you are not allowed to do anything,' she continues. 'Not even picnic.' So, in a subversive gesture, Jongerius made a picnic cloth on which she printed a map of the park and highlighted good potential picnic spots. She also designed a raincoat covered with German sayings about rain, as well as some brightly coloured packaging to be used by the shops. 'It's so grey and depressing there that I wanted to cheer everyone up,' she says.

In order to give the region a certain identity, Wanders dreamed up cookies and a loaf of bread in the form of the wooden boxes in which orange trees are planted. He hopes that the region's bakers will

there were once 550 orange trees. Jongerius made a book of orange recipes. Guixé developed an orange peeler, as well as a lollipop with an orange pip at its centre. 'When you've finished it, you can put the pip in the earth. Five years later, you have an orange tree,' he says.

The park itself proved a rich source of ideas. Bey made seats out of hay, bark and hedges. He added the backs of antique chairs to tree trunks to create benches. Guixé came up with a vase whose outer glass cavity is filled with earth. In the inner one, the flowers sit in water. He also invented a 'smell catcher', which is made from paper used in the perfume industry. 'If you put the paper near a flower, it catches its scent,' he says.

adopt them as local specialities.

So far, Italian manufacturers have expressed interest in producing several of the products. Weiss and Ramakers, however, are hoping to find industrial partners in Dessau-Wörlitz who can ensure international distribution.

'Our motto is "Act local, think global",' says Ramakers. 'The whole idea is to do something for the region, inspired by the region, but not to be provincial. We want the products to be sold all over the world.'

For more information about the Dessau-Wörlitz Third International Garden Festival, which runs until 5 September, call 00 49 340 646150. Droog products are available at Same, 146 Brick Lane, London E1 (inquiries 0171 247 9992). 'Droog Design Couleur Locale' is published by Orange Square at £14.50

Photographs **Marsel Loermans**

Personal Planner 2000 for WE The Dutch clothing company WE approaches Droog to design a special product to distinguish itself as a strong brand. It could be anything except clothing. Studio Mevis & Van Deursen designs a personal planner that can be adapted to the user's taste.

The cover consists of transparent soft plastic with lots of places to store all kinds of small personal belongings, for users to create and change the look of their own, truly personal planner.

Playhouse Droog Design asked Traast & Gruson to participate in the Playhouse project for Bang & Olufsen. These designers create a life size wire frame house made of fluorescent metal tubes. By activating the B&O products, integrated in this structure, visitors can experience a lively house.

Images on a TV screen suggest the presence of a bathroom and sounds from a CD player evoke associations with the kitchen. Only a few visitors dared to pick up the ringing phone.

Data Treasures New York Times magazine organizes a competition to design a time capsule to be opened 1000 years from now to reveal what living in this day and age is all about. Jurgen Bey takes part for Droog Design.

Instead of designing a capsule, a piece of hardware in which material will be preserved, Bey prefers to go beyond the box.

His idea is that we should transmit information to the future in an organic way, not unlike the manner in which we now get data from the past, by excavation and heritage. This process should be continued by providing contemporary products with information on our culture and by having them survive in a natural process, which implies that circumstances decide which products will survive 1000 years. The data and products are divided into three groups: Medical and scientific data to be engraved by laser into human implantations, teeth, pacemakers, and other artificial additions to the human body. Information on our popular culture should be added to Coca Cola tins and bottles. The texts and images have to inform future generations about us. Personal information, the last kind, should be etched photographically into beloved objects. In the year 3000 all the objects with different kinds of information are to be recovered.

The entry does not win. This is no unexpected disappointment, since beforehand the panel that formulated the conditions, had stated that prospective designers could think 'outside the box' but that such entries couldn't be carried out. But the jury appreciates Jurgen Bey's entry and so it is published in The New York Times Magazine in December 1999.

The New York Times Magazine, December 5, 1999
JURGEN BEY FOR DROOG DESIGN

When the Dutch collective known as Droog Design considered what things last for centuries, its members settled on three categories: heirlooms, trash and tombs. Jurgen Bey, one of Droog's members, proposes piggybacking capsule data on all three forms. The most arresting of these involves using human bodies as time capsules.

That alone is nothing new: mummified corpses have long yielded a treasure of

CULTURAL DATA TREASURE
01-01-3000 AC
44°42'N 47°01'W

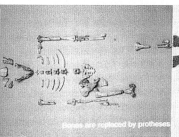
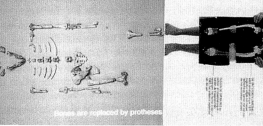

Bey's strategy (from left): Bones that could be replaced by prostheses;

Mandarina Duck bags Droog is commissioned by the Italian Company Mandarina Duck to design a series of technical bags. Several designers participate in this project.
The company chooses Marcel Wanders' concept. It is based on an inflated shape with integrated belt. The technical development of this innovative concept takes a few years. In the end it turns out to be very difficult to realize the original idea. On his own initiative Marcel Wanders continues the process with the company. The result is introduced on the market in 2002.

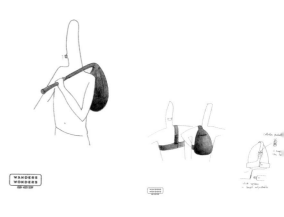

SO by Alexander van Slobbe presents an exhibition on Droog Design

DutchDroogDesign

DroogDesign
Peter van der Jagt
Doorbell Bottoms Up / dmd 62
Stainless steel
and crystal

Exhibition / SO / Joi'x Corporation
Tokyo, February 20-28

Invitation and catalogue,
design Experimental Jetset

DroogDesign
Arnout Visser
Salad Sunrise / dmd 11
Pyrex glass

Droog Design for Documenta XI Okwui Enwezor, artistic director of Documenta XI, 2002 in Kassel, organizes a pitch for the design of the logo of this event. Droog Design is selected as one of six studios. The keywords given by Enwezor are: Globalisation of modern art and interdisciplinariness of the artists. Droog Design invites Studio Gonnissen en Widdershoven (now Thonik) to participate in this project. Gonnissen en Widdershoven consider a T-shirt to be an omnipresent medium and propose to apply it as a logo. Their proposal is a T-shirt, imprinted with two vertical stripes forming the number 11. It is to be distributed worldwide. Its recipients should then send back photographs of themselves wearing the shirt. The pictures are to be used as house style items on book covers, brochures, banners and other items to provide the large art manifestation with graphic identity. This proposal is explained in a booklet, an image essay.

Enwezor's first reaction is positive 'An unexpected proposal. In this age of extreme violence it is good to focus on the body. That's what I like about the concept of the T-shirt'. However, he finally chooses the entry of the Austrian designer Ecce Bonk.

Folding bookcase by Konings & Bey, 1991 **Powerpoint** by Hopman, 1995 **Drawing Table** by Opske de Jong, 1990

Washbasin by Dick van Hoff, 1997 'The Cross' Bench by Hutten, 1994 **Chair with holes** by Gijs Bakker, 1989

Monument, 1999

Chest of Drawers 'You can't lay down your memories' by Tejo Remy was designed in 1991. It trains your memory, you have to remember exactly what went into which drawer. The *** designed by Hella Jongerius in 1995 exploits the air bubbles in the material as an aesthetic element and takes a new look on an existing form in a new material.

"By cross-breeding and grafting, products and functions of a different nature can merge and develop into new products".

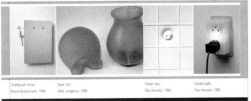

Toothbrush mirror, Roland Butschmann, 1995 | Vase 'Urn', Hella Jongerius, 1996 | Power tiles, Paul Hessels, 1995 | Socket light, Paul Hessels, 1995

>1995

shaken, not stirred

Holland holds a special place in the European imagination. The Low Lands. The stoic free-thinkers fighting back the chilly waters of the North Sea and the cultural conservatism of their neighbours. State-regulated prostitution. Homosexual unions. Euthanasia. And of course, all that legalised marijuana. In design terms, Holland occupies a particular place as well. France still labours under *beaux arts* allusions to *bon gout*. In Italy, Memphis has dissolved into a mis-guided mannerism, its expensive one-offs now holed up in the homes of Cote d'Azur fashion photographers. Spain has all but bleeped the radar, as Maraschal's cute Barcelona Olympic's logo fades on a thousand t-shirts in cupboards around the world. And

England, well, England still can't seem to decide whether it *really* believes in the brow-knitted rigour of Tom Dixon's aesthetics or the fantasy fittings of an Avengers futurism. Either way, fuelled on by *Wallpaper*, Tyler Brulé's style-bible for 'good living' — and all the quick copy jobs being pulled off in everything from *Elle Decor* to *Feng Shui Living* — London is about to drown itself in its own hype.

Meanwhile, Holland carries on. With that notorious light, you get the feel-ing Vermeer could still happily roam those flat, fluro-green, geometrically arranged fields with their transparent cubic glass-houses shining into the night. And with their particular design aesthetic it's as if Mondrian, Rietveld and Van Doesberg still loiter in the

"macramé meets high-tech". The **Knotted chair** by Marcel Wanders was created in 1996 during the Dry Tech workshop at the Aviation and Space Lab at Delft University of Technology.

"Workshops are an important part of our activities, they stimulate the interaction between creative design work and the reality of production."

2000

Presentation Milan, March 21-25

New Designs

Jaap van Arkel, Gijs Bakker, Timo Breumelhof, Peter Hopman, Richard Hutten, Peter van der Jagt, Hella Jongerius, Stijn Roodnat, Hector Serrano, Chris Slutter, Arnout Visser and Erik Jan Kwakkel, Jesse Visser

+

Do Create

Thomas Bernstrand, Jurgen Bey, Dawn Finley, Martí Guixé, Dick van Hoff, Marijn van der Poll, Radi Designers, Frank Tjepkema and Peter van der Jagt, Bas van Tol, Thomas Widdershoven and Dinie Besems

+

Indigo, Droog Design for Levi's RED

Jurgen Bey

do + Droog Design = do create

You are invited to join do and Droog Design at the 'do create' exhibition, during the International Furniture Fair 2000 in Milan. do create will present a series of products made for do, an ever-changing brand that depends on what you do. These products will challenge you to play, communicate, hit, switch, talk, walk, run, stick and interact. All 'do create' needs to complete the exhibition is you.

>do create dates:
tuesday 11th to sunday 16th of april 2000
opening hours: 11.00 - 21.00
do create opening party: tuesday 11th, 19.00 - 22.00

>do create address:
Spazio la Posteria
Via G. Sacchi 5/7
20121 Milan
T: + 39 (0)2 86 46 15 47
F: + 39 (0)2 86 46 02 50

>do creators:
Thomas Bernstrand, Jurgen Bey, Dawn Finley, Martí Guixé, Dick van Hoff, Marijn van der Poll, Radi Designers, Frank Tjepkema & Peter van der Jagt, Thomas Widdershoven & Dinie Besems, Bas van Tol.

do stick	do create	do cut	do swing
do post	do connect	do scratch	do kiss
do break	do dance	do smash	do eat

For more information about do create: visit http://www.dosurf.com or mail to domail@dosurf.com

do > lauriergracht 39. 1016 rg amsterdam. p.o.box 3240. 1011 aa amsterdam. the netherlands.
T. +31 (0)20 5301070. F. +31 (0)20 5301061.
Stichting Droog Design > damrak 265. 1012 zj amsterdam. the netherlands.
T+31 (0)20 6269809. F+31 (0)20 6388828. e-mail: droog@euronet.nl. internet: www.droogdesign.nl

DROOG
DESIGN
CATALOGUE

After selecting products made by young Dutch designers, and proceeding by additionally initiating their own projects for which they select designers, the obvious next step for Droog Design was to take on commissions from institutions and companies. Now Droog Design operates as an ever changing but controlled network, doing all three. Especially the commission part of Droog Design shows a remarkable shift in emphasis from the tangible object towards the immaterial: companies rather unexpectedly ask Droog Design to make a contribution to their identity instead of their product range. Now this requires a completely different approach towards what needs to be created. Products cannot serve as a vehicle to present fresh and sometimes controversial ideas about design any longer. Rather they are the stimuli to new brand-related experiences.

NRC Handelsblad,
May 31, 2000

do + Droog Design = do Create Publicity firm KesselsKramer in Amsterdam has created a totally empty brand - a brand without product or service -, called do. It presupposes consumer interaction. The meaning of do can be anything, as long as there is consumer activity and consumer interpretation.
Droog Design proposes to design products for do. The project do Create is born.
For Droog Design, designing a range of products for KesselsKramer's brand do means intensification of their own starting point and giving different views of the notion of personal production which is becoming more and more en vogue these days.
Within the do Create project consumers are invited to interact and play, and thereby influence the design. You buy an experience: it is what you do to the object or what the object does to you that counts.
The range of do - products, including a steel cubic chair by Marijn van der Pol that has to be hammered into shape, is first shown in Spazio La Posteria in Milan, during the International Furniture Fair. Then it travels to Rotterdam, Paris, Tokyo, London and as part of 'do Apartment' to New York. The installation designed by Bas van Tol consists of many doors in different colours, serving as information panel, pedestal or any other functions needed there and then.

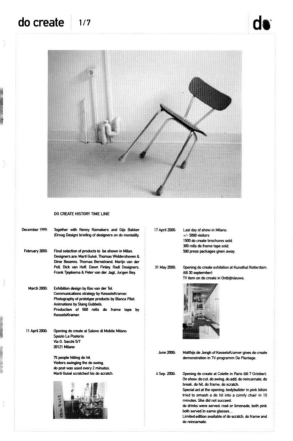

do create | 1/7

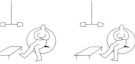

Instructions for do connect and do swing

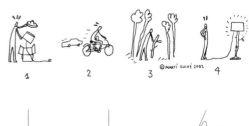

Instruction for do scratch

USER VIEW

Sketch for do post,
Dawn Finley

Wieke

Van: Info <info@droogdesign.nl>
Aan: Renny Ramakers <renny@droogdesign.nl>; <gijs@droogdesign.nl>; Astrid Honold <astrid@droogdesign.nl>; wieke gerrits <wieke@droogdesign.nl>
Verzonden: donderdag 19 april 2001 11:36
Onderwerp: Fw: example of do frame

----- Original Message -----
From: do create
To: caligari@kesselskramer.nl
Cc: Catelijne@invent.nl ; droog@euronet.nl ; gina@theapt.com ; poels@attglobal.net ; dvdveld@pop.dds.nl ; magiver@kesselskramer.nl ; gun@kesselskramer.nl
Sent: Thursday, April 19, 2001 12:35 PM
Subject: example of do frame

your car. Someone broke into a car of a visitor at the Salone in Milan. But they were happy that they just bought 'do frame'.. With do greetings, Joanna

Sketch for do frame, Martí Guíxé

The Independant on Sunday,
May 14, 2000

Sketches do break,
Frank Tjepkema &
Peter van der Jagt

225

DESIGN

fig.1   fig.2   fig.3

mashing ideas

ssembling flatpack shelves is the
sest most people get to interacting
h their furniture. But one of
world's most sophisticated design
ups has plans to change all that.
na Rattray gets hooked on Droog

Thwunk. Pause. Thwunk. The reverent
hush of the gallery is broken. The smart
Milanese may be feigning nonchalance,
but with each deafening reverberation,
you can see that their curiosity is being aroused.
  Design shows are usually quiet affairs.
Furniture isn't supposed to do anything apart
from sit there and be used, or finished maybe.
But this show is different. The sound you can
hear is that of a hollow cube of steel being
whacked by a man with a sledgehammer. And so,
this isn't anger management, or industrial sabo-
tage by a jealous designer – this is the sound of a
chair being born.
  The do-it-yourself chair is part of a new project
by the influential Dutch design group, Droog.
Launched at the recent Milan Furniture Fair –
the design world's equivalent of fashion week –
the Do Create range features pieces by international designers which invite – or, more appropri-
ately, demand – participation from the user.
  Droog's design credentials are about as cool as
you can get. From the 1991 You Can't Lay Down
Your Memories chest of drawers by Tejo Remy,
which scrapped together old drawer fronts in new
casings in a jumbled bundle, to the 1996 Knotted
Chair by Marcel Wanders, which succeeded in
turning limp rope into a solid structure, Droog
has successfully identified designers whose work
challenges the status quo and provokes new levels
of thought and material usage. For this latest project, Droog (the name comes from A Clockwork
Orange) joined force with Do – a kind of textual
experiment initiated three years ago by the
impossibly inventive Dutch advertising agency
KesselsKramer.
  As well as the Do I hit chair, which is by Dutch
designer Marijn van der Poll, there is Marti
Guixé's Scratch light – so called because to use it
you have to scratch the black paint off to let the

light shine through. The Spanish designer is also
responsible for the Link standard light. You buy
the shade, the stand and the light fitting but you
have to improvise the "pole" which joins them all
together: it could be a tree branch, a stack of cans,
a small child – it's entirely up to you. Jurgen Bey's
Do Add chairs are even stranger. Made from
chrome-plated steel and laminate, each chair has
what Bey calls a "handicap". The first has one leg
shorter than the others, the second has a side-
ways-extended seat. Each requires some personal
intervention in order to fulfil its promise of use.
So, for the short-legged chair you need a prop, a
pile of books, say, to make it function. For the
"stunt" chair, you need another person, or yet
another pile of books, to serve as a counter-
balance and stop you toppling over.
  This may all seem a bit daft. After all, the one
thing everyone knows about design is that, before
anything else, products are supposed to work.
And the function of a chair, you might say, is to be
sat on without falling over. But Bey shares
Droog's belief that design is about more than ▶

2'

INDEPENDENT ON SUNDAY 14 May 2000

Instructions for do hit and do break

Influential Dutch design
group Droog joined
forces with experiments
brand Do for its latest
project – Do Create.
This features designs
which demand
interaction on the part
of the user. The Do hit
chair, above, by Marijn
van der Poll, is one of
this pieces which are
documented in a series
of photographs by
Hidde Kalkhoven for
Droog launched other
new pieces, including
the Wallpaper lamp by

Post graduate The master-program at the
Design Academy in Eindhoven has been
reorganised. The new set up is called 3i-masters,
an industrial/interior/identity design cluster
that consists of three overlapping studios.
Studio Edelcoort is asked to take care of
identity. Studio Merkx/Giraud is asked to lead
the interior studio. Droog Design is requested
to lead the industrial design studio.
Renny Ramakers will focus on reflection and
contextualisation of product design. Gijs Bakker,
already a teacher in the regular course, aims
to go into the essence of existence.

Kölner Klopfer Students at the Fachhochschule
Köln in Germany award Droog Design the fourth
'Kölner Klopfer', the design equivalent of Bambi.
The wobbly golden rabbit made of rubber is
handed to Renny Ramakers on January 18th
together with a bouquet of carrots.

Mandarina Duck flagship store, Paris Mandarina Duck, Italian manufacturer and sales company for bags, clothing and accessories, assigns Droog Design the task of designing their flagship store at fancy Rue Saint Honoré in Paris. The company allows Droog exceptional freedom. Droog Design asks NL Architects to do this commission. They have weekly meetings during one year.

The interior differs from the usual coherence of form, material and colour. NL Architects develop several installations, each triggering a different experience. The underlying idea is hitched to the original commission by Mandarina Duck that changed during the process. The brief called for an interior that could be used in a series of stores. The different branches are to have the same resonance and yet be distinguishable from each other. The proposal made for Mandarina Duck is a catalogue of furnishing units, in which to display the merchandise. For each location a different choice can be made with the possibility of exchanging items between branches.

The store opens in 2000 and unfortunately closes again almost two years later. Mandarina Duck keeps the installations stored and still has plans to use them again.

Invitation			Invitation
	0h00	26	219,
		20h30	75001
	Invitation	à	Architects
	Baptême	Boutique:	Concept
	de	de	Design/
	Droog	Duck:	et
	flagship	Honoré	Jeudi
	Kid	l'ère	Loco
	Mandarina	Musiques:	NL
	nouveau	Invitation	octobre,
	Paris	Patrick	rue
	Saint	Vidal	

Invitation for the opening, sheet of stickers, design Experimental Jetset

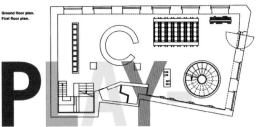

PLAY GROUND

Ground floor plan.
First floor plan.

IN THE PARIS SHOP THAT NL ARCHITECTS DESIGNED FOR MANDARINA DUCK, YOU PLAY HIDE-AND-SEEK IN SEARCH OF THINGS TO BUY. BY CHRIS SCOTT. PHOTOGRAPHY BY WOUTER. STYLING BY ERJAN BORR

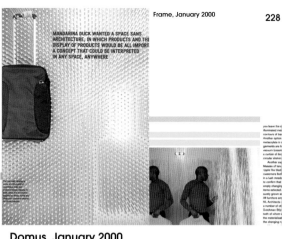

MANDARINA DUCK WANTED A SPACE SANS ARCHITECTURE, IN WHICH PRODUCTS AND THE DISPLAY OF PRODUCTS WOULD BE ALL IMPORT A CONCEPT THAT COULD BE INTERPRETED IN ANY SPACE, ANYWHERE

Domus, January 2000

Droog and Duck

Francesca Picchi sul negozio di Parigi per Mandarina Duck

Francesca Picchi on the new store for Mandarina Duck in Paris

Fotografie di/ Photography by Christoph Kircherer

Interior Design, April 2002

determined manner. Mobile and temporary furniture and fixtures facilitate this sense of free transition and shifting options. But the store's single permanent element, a spiral staircase between the two floors, also works to create the feeling of motion and rapid transition: ►

shopping as a form of entertainment and this is its main attraction.

PHOTOGRAPHY: CHRISTOPH KICHERER

Droog Design wins Kho Liang Ie award

On September 7th Amsterdam cultural councillor Saskia Bruines presents Droog Design with the Kho Liang Ie award for Industrial Design. It is one of 18 annual prizes awarded by the city c Amsterdam. The reason Droog Design gets it is their seventh presentation in Milan. From the jury report: 'Droog Design has influenced, and still influences the Dutch design climate. Droog Design catches signals, encourages experiments and development, guides debate and reflection, creates conditions and recognises the importance of image building and the way the market works. Droog Design builds bridges, creates links and is an intermediary and a protagonist. Droog Design deserves the Kho Liang Ie Award for its continuing vitality. The in many ways different seventh presentation in Milan, in the spring of 1999, at three different locations, was an unmistakable proof of this vitality'.
Jury members are Paul Mertz, Cok de Rooy and Marcel Wanders.

uitreiking Kho Liang Ie prijs
juni 2000, Amsterdam
photo: A. HONOLD

Peters, v. Hoff, Widdershoven, Bakker, Ramakers, v. Eijk,
Gonnissen, Bey, v. Arkel, Karposhoek, Jongerius,
de Wolff & Boelstra (DMD), Hutten, Brekveld,
Oosterhof, Visser, Kwakkel, Smeets

De naam Droog Design weerspiegelt perfect. Hij verenigt het straffe, het Spartaanse met de sprankeling, de luchtigheid en de milde zelfspot, die voor het eerst een glimlach toestaan. Op 28 februari 1994 richten Ramakers en Gijs Bakker de Stichting Droog Design op. Die is ongekend actief. Eigen exposities, van Keulen en Rotterdam tot Helsinki, Parijs en Frankfurt. Participatie in manifestaties, van Bremen tot Utrecht, van Londen tot Montreal en New York. Vermelding in jaarboeken, aanwezigheid in het museumcafé van het Moma, samenwerking met velen. Producenten, distributeurs, buitenlandse fabrikanten, geestverwanten.

Met het aantal Droog Designers groeit de verscheidenheid, terwijl de eenheid blijft. 'Spirit of the Nineties' schrijft Ramakers in een beeldende bundel uit 1998. Wie het verzamelwerk Holland in vorm (slechts elf jaar ouder) ernaast legt, merkt, ziet, voelt hoe fris de noordenwind is. De bries blaast onverminderd.

Droog Design heeft het Nederlandse ontwerpklimaat beïnvloed en doet dat nog. Droog Design vangt signalen op, stimuleert experiment en ontwikkeling, spoort aan tot debat en reflectie, schept voorwaarden, onderkent de betekenis van beeldvorming en marktwerking. Droog Design legt bruggen en connecties, is intermediair en protagonist. Website en nieuwsbrief informeren en enthousiasmeren, boeken documenteren.

De jury heeft grote bewondering voor het idee achter Droog en voor het vele dat de kleine organisatie heeft verricht, begeleid en teweeggebracht. Zij verwelkomt recente plannen als de toenadering tot het kunstvakonderwijs en de overschrijding van disciplines. Daarnaast roemt zij de Droog Designers, om wie uiteindelijk alles draait. Vormgevers, ontwerpers, in diverse stadia van beroepsuitoefening die, met behoud van hun eigen identiteit, inhoud gaven en geven aan een nieuwe mentaliteit en gezamenlijk een indrukwekkend oeuvre hebben opgebouwd dat terecht alom waardering oogstte en oogst.

Indigo, retail installation for Levi's RED Levi's RED commissions Droog Design for a windows concept to be presented in a few high end shops in different parts of the world. Droog Design asks Jurgen Bey to participate in this project.

Jurgen Bey bases his design on the fact that the originally colourless indigo plant reveals its special blue colour by a chemical reaction with water. Not immediately, but slowly the colour changes into the deepest blue. His idea is to show the Levi's RED Line behind a screen, shifting between transparent and indigo blue. This is the start of a process in which different kinds of possibilities are investigated. The result is an installation in which the latest liquid crystal technology is applied. The pulsating screen is first shown at the Fashion Week in February at Jones' in London and at Colette in Paris. Droog Design shows Indigo in Milan during the International Furniture Fair. Afterwards, the installation visits several major cities all over the world.

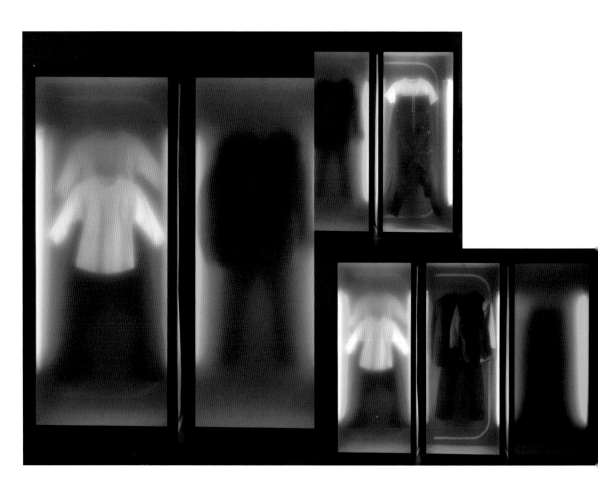

The real life of objects, Droog Design in use

Trevor Cromie of the Lighthouse Trust in Glasgow organizes a very special exhibition about Droog Design. In the period prior to the exhibition, Droog products are lodged with six Glaswegian households. A round the clock video diary is made of this stay. Quite surprising is the intensive and multifunctional product use. Martijn Hoogendijk's pallet, for instance, is laid and sat upon and put in all kinds of positions as a toy for children. The Lighthouse produces the interactive dvd publication 'The real life of objects' to document the project.

Mandy Mackintosh
Govanhill, G43

The Utrecht Central Museum has supplemented its large collection of Droog Design products and updated it to 1999. The museum organizes a travelling exhibition.
Part of the Droog tour organized by the Utrecht Central Museum is a visit to Tokyo.
Approximately 15.000 people visit the Ozone Living Design Centre where the Droog collection is combined with Dutch fashion.

2001

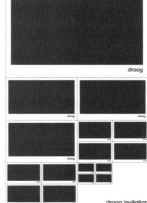

droog non id, design
Jop van Bennekom

droog invitation

Presentation Milan, April 3-8

Me, Myself and You
Alias Vollaers-Zwart, Jop van Bennekom,
Nina Farkache, Moniek Gerner, Martí
Guixé, Kummer & Herman, Next Architects,
Re-Magazine/Misha de Ridder
+
Dry Kitchen
Fernando Brizio, Peter van der Jagt, Erik Jan
Kwakkel, Arnout Visser, Ton Matton/Schie 2.0,
Noriko Yasuda
+
Pocket Furniture, Droog Design for Picus
Joost Grootens, Richard Hutten, Jan Konings,
Joseph Plateau graphic designers, Wieki Somers
and Dylan van den Berg

Achille Castiglioni in
private rocking chair,
Martí Guixé

private rocking chair

Martí Guixé
2001
birch plywood
lacquered, textile
150 x 140 x 84 cm

private chair

Martí Guixé
2001
birch plywood, lacquered
140 x 100 x 58 cm

Me, Myself and You, human contact in the 21st century Human interaction is the basic theme of the project Me, Myself and You. It deals with the way in which designed objects influence social behaviour, the perception of personal identity and the experience of communication. It is a matter of including yourself in or secluding yourself from your surroundings. A wide range of opportunities reveals itself. Furniture can provide isolation as well as stimulate playful togetherness.

In Martí Guixé's private chair and private rocking chair one can become invisible in a crowded space. The same is true for the table playground by Moniek Gerner. Underneath a table children can have their own secret world using the hooks under the table. Next Architects designed two doors that guarantee complete privacy. The other designs generate contact between users. Next Architects designs a series of fences that can be used together and shared between neighbours. The bench Come a little bit closer, by Nina Farkache, featuring discs that slide on marbles, is about gentle collision into relations and human contact.

The project is shown in Milan, again in Spazio La Posteria during the International Furniture Fair. The installation is designed by Alias. They cover the floor with fields of coloured cards that can be taken away by visitors as exhibition souvenirs. Especially for this occasion Jop van Bennekom designs a so called droog non id logo that is applied to all communication products, including bags and T-shirts.

me, myself and you

**Dit
is
van
mij,**

**laat
me
met
rust**

Spy hole door

Next Architects
2001
synthetics
85 x 212 x 8 cm

Key hole door

Next Architects
2001
steel
85 x 212 x 8 cm

De 'Private Rocking Chair' van Marti Guixi en de schuttingen van Next Architects. Te zien in de Kunsthal, Rotterdam.

Dry Kitchen At the Fair in Milan, Droog Design shows two kitchens. Both are designed according to the mentality of Droog Design, yet the outcome is entirely different.

The tile kitchen by Arnout Visser, Erik Jan Kwakkel and Peter van der Jagt is based upon a building system of ordinary tiles. They have added a number of special tiles in which several functions have been integrated. Ingenuously shaped ones serve to build round corners and a basin. It can be considered an extension to the bathroom tiles they did earlier on.

Ton Matton (then member of Schie 2.0) designs an autarkic kitchen. It is freed from its architectural context and can function in any space as an autonomous piece of furniture. Environmental principles fort self-support are applied and visualize the process of cooling, wastewater treatment and composting.

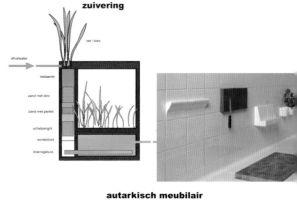

zuivering

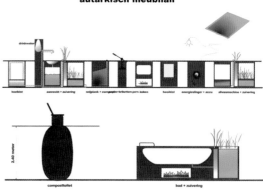

autarkisch meubilair

Pocket Furniture, Droog Design for Picus Dutch cigar box manufacturer Picus used to produce mainly anonymous cheap wooden cigar packaging, with an additional luxury line of exclusive, beautifully finished humidors for affluent smokers. Since the market for cigar boxes has become difficult, they decide to initiate a new type of product. Picus commissions Droog Design to develop new concepts to exploit its high quality production expertise.

Droog Design selects four designers to create a new line of boxes, serving different purposes. The box as a container in the broadest sense of the word becomes the central issue. The material is predominantly wood. The designers work with four entirely different approaches to this project. They generate personal concepts that have one thing in common: their cigar box roots.

Richard Hutten creates a series of maple boxes with functional extras in the lids, that underline their use. Joost Grootens chooses to explore the border between the box as an object and as packaging, resulting in a series of boxes with a function strikingly identical to that of the object inside. Jan Konings makes the chest box, a combination of a large number of boxes that can be assembled in different and unique configurations. Wieki Somers together with Dylan van den Berg stays very close to the cigar box, she chooses to radically stretch it to the size of furniture, including the hinges, locks and even the printed paper along the edges.

Pocket furniture
Droog Design for Picus

Wieki Somers and Dylan van den Berg, sketch for cigar box wardrobe

Stamp box

Richard Hutten
maple MDF, maple
46 x 12,2 x 4,4 cm

Drawing box

Richard Hutten
maple MDF
32,8 x 18 x 8,5 cm

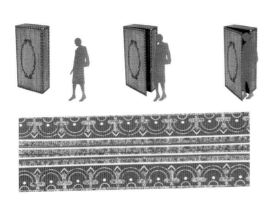

Chest box

Jan Konings
birch plywood
60 x 60 x 40 cm

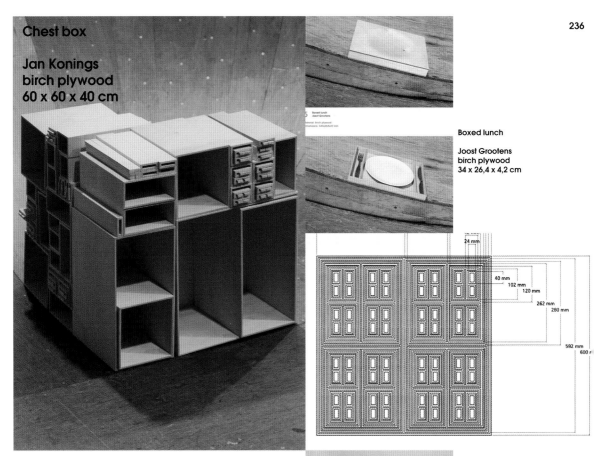

Boxed lunch

Joost Grootens
birch plywood
34 x 26,4 x 4,2 cm

Videorom, El Mundo Nuevo Valencia Biennial

Valencia's first biennial for fine arts in 2001 commissions Droog Design to propose a way to present video art in the streets. During the 123 days of the Biennale videos of 123 international artists to be shown in the 'Videorom' should travel around to reach different places in and around the city. Referring to the Biennial's theme 'seven virtues and vices' Studio Traast & Gruson develop a concept for a number of tents in which videos can be played. According to this concept, videos selected based on 'vice' must be shown at places that are characterized by 'virtue' such as churches. The 'virtue' videos should be displayed at places like nightclubs. Skaters in specially designed costumes are supposed to hang around and to hand information to passers by. The Biennale chooses to have only one bigger tent.

System Almighty, 010101 - Art in Technological Times, SF MOMA

The San Francisco Museum of Modern Art (SF MOMA) organizes an exhibition about new developments in art, architecture and design and their evolution in a world altered by the increasing presence of digital media and technology. Droog Design is asked to contribute with an installation. The starting point for the project 'System Almighty' is the network community our society has turned into. The installation consists of three parts: the first shows a picture by Ries Straver symbolizing mankind as a system extension. The second is dedicated to 'the intangibility of the system': a screen with 15000 four-letter words, only made visible with the help of visitor operated hair dryers. This part is designed by Matijs Korpershoek, Thonik and Ed van Hinte. The theme of part three, 'the system can be disordered', by Lauran Schijvens works with a Barcode scanner. On the outside wall of a large transparant orange box containing all kinds of household appliances and electric Droog products, the public can scan any barcode they have with them, for instance on one's driving license. This results in several seconds of household action by four items in the box. The combination depends on the barcode, but cannot be predicted in advance.

Hybrid, Droog Design for Hoogstad Architects The Dutch architect Jan Hoogstad has designed highrise buildings based on off-shore constructions. The principle of the 'hybrid' consists of a durable core that enables flexible interior design and facades with a relatively short lifespan. Hoogstad approaches Droog Design for proposals for such a mantle. The project is to be presented in several metropoles, like Buenos Aires and Tokyo.

Jurgen Bey, Alias and Frank Tjepkema's Studio Open develop ideas. Alias' concept is based upon the interference of two linear patterns, one to be put on the inside construction and one on the mantle. A moiré effect will result. Studio Open takes weaving as a starting point. Every function or use in the mantle must have its own colour and together they form an ever changing pattern. In Jurgen Bey's proposal the mantle influences the volume of the building by using fine or rough meshes depending on user needs. The project is abandoned because of 9/11.

Wall - Filter
Pared - Filtro

Zoo - Office
Jardín Zoóligico - Oficina

Insight
Dentro

Villa Droog Villa Noailles in Hyères is an enormous villa, with a style somewhere in between functionalism and Art Deco, designed by Robert Mallet Stevens in 1923. It used to be a lively meeting place for artists such as Jean Cocteau and Theo van Doesburg who were invited by the rich and generous owners Mr and Mrs Noailles to spend the summer working on their latest ideas.

Jean Pierre Blanc, who over the last few years revitalized the villa as a cultural hotspot, asks Droog to do an exhibition there. Renny Ramakers decides not to use the regular exhibition space in the basement but to bring the empty villa to life again. All the rooms are furnished with Droog products. Photographs of the former residents are part of the exhibition.

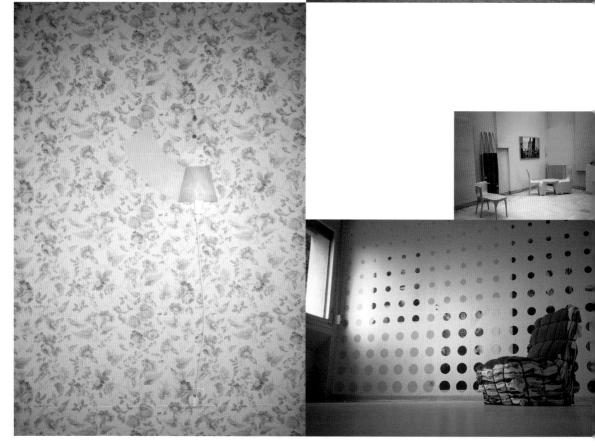

Levi's again The project with Levi's continues. Jurgen Bey designs another window concept for Levi's RED. He also develops packaging that can be used as a tablecloth. Frank Tjepkema and John Maatman come up with an idea to attract attention in the shops: a vacuum sealed pair of jeans on a clothes hanger.

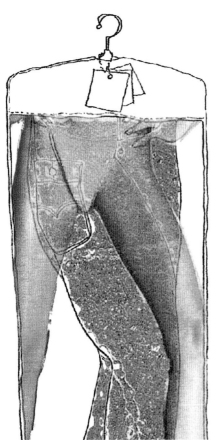

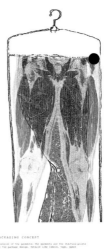

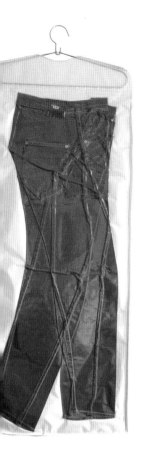

Weekend Financial Times, how to spend it, February 2001

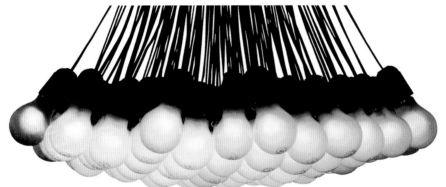

Droog: what's the big idea?

It's the closest thing design has to punk rock or Pop Art. Helen Kirwan-Taylor visits Droog, the heavily ironic Dutch design group where no idea is too wild or unsellable to be considered.

15

2002

Presentation Milan, April 10-14

Real Life Revisited, Hotel Droog ★
Emmy Blok, Franck Bragigand, Nina Farkache,
Joost Grootens, Cynthia Hathaway, Han
Koning, Matijs Korpershoek, Egbert-Jan Lam,
Louise Maniette, Tarmo Piirmets, Tet Reuver,
Floris Schiferli, Hector Serrano, Paolo Ulian,
Jet Vervest, Noriko Yasuda
+
Real Life Revisited, Restoring daily life
Franck Bragigand
+
Less + More, Droog Design in context
Thonik
+
Droog Shop
Richard Hutten

Real life revisited The title of Droog's tenth presentation during the International Furniture Fair is 'Real life revisited'. In an environment where all eyes are perpetually focused on slickly styled products and 'new' is embraced just for the sake of it, Droog Design looks for everyday life situations where the number of new products is kept to a minimum. It is about integration of the new and the existing, the special and the common, the ugly and the beautiful, perfection and imperfection, illusion and reality. For the duration of the fair, artist Franck Bragigand, who designates his art as painting mass production and the garbage of society, paints used and unused objects brought in by visitors to the exhibition space at Via Lomazzo.

A shabby one-star hotel on Via Mercato is temporarily renamed Hotel Droog ☆. At first sight everything is what it used to be. No real changes have been made to the hotel's interior, but in each room something is added by the participating designers. The focus is neither on the space itself, nor on creating yet another design hotel, but on transforming this cheap place into an extraordinary experience with just a few additions. People flock to see it. Some six thousand visitors jostle through its 12 rooms. The queue at the entrance grows as the word spreads. A key to this success is a passport made by Daniel van der Velden and Maureen Mooren. Instead of handing over their passports for examination, visitors are offered one to take on a new identity. The passport functions also as a catalogue. Logo's of the various designs can be stamped on the pages. Amazingly the hotel is actually appreciated for its shoddy cheapness. People think the standard hotel interior is a design project. Each lamp and cupboard is closely inspected. Certain modifications are so minimal that they aren't noticed. Sometimes even the 'wrong' object receives praise.

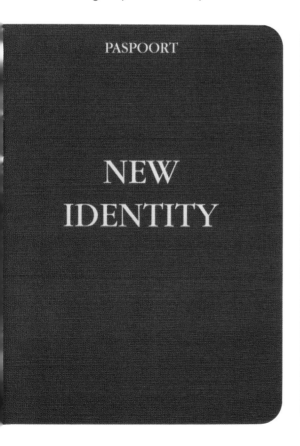

Floris Schiferli
(M.Masters,Eindhoven)
'Sit down, gentlemen/Respect the cleaning woman'

Casa Brutus, July 2002

ドローグ・デザインが開業し
1ツ星ホテルの実態は？

Droog Design

サローネ本会場の「グランドホテル・サローネ」に対抗しての企画なのか？
ミラノに実際にあるホテルに手を加えた、とってもドローグなデザイン・ホテル。
たった5日間の期間限定「ホテル・ドローグ」を案内しましょう。
photo_Fendry Ekel

JULY 2002

Project Restoring Daily Life,
Frank Bragigand

de Volkskrant · donderdag 23 mei 2002   17K

Oprichters van Droog Design houden niet van achterom kijken

DROOG DID IT AGAIN

Droog Design bestaat tien jaar. Geen reden voor een groot feest, vinden oprichters Gijs Bakker en Renny Ramakers. Ze kijken liever vooruit. 'Het mag geen verkopen van lucht worden.' Door Jeroen Junte

Een bloembol verpakt in gedroogde koeienmest, een vinding van Andreas Möller uit 1994, is helemaal conform de Droog-doctrine.

Andreas Möller: Bulb bag, 1994

MILAN, 10 - 14 APRIL 2002★

For the duration of the Salone del mobile 2002, a shabby one-star hotel on the Via delle Erbe in Milan was renamed Hotel droog★. People flocked to see it; some six thousand visitors jostled through its 12 rooms.

Hotel droog★ distances itself from the phenomenon design hotel or art hotel. At first glance, the hotel appears as it always had. Just a few additions transform the hotel into a special experience.

Hotel droog★

A videowork of Fendry Ekel for Droog Design
Available on DVD and VHS
Published by Droog Design

© Droog Design/Fendry Ekel 2002

Hotel droog★ · VIDEO TAPE · 2002

Intermediair, June 6, 2002

werk & leven

Kleerhanger met lamp in Milanese hotelkamer, Hector Serrano

Droog genoeg?

NEDERLANDS DESIGN VEROVERT DE WERELD

De bekendheid van het Nederlandse Droog Design reikt tot over de grenzen. De lamp met 85 peertjes en de sloophoutkasten zijn wereldberoemd. Tegelijk weet niemand wat Droog precies is. Een bedrijf? Een merk? Of een platform voor jonge ontwerpers?

DOOR DIDO MICHIELSEN

Paolo Ulian badmat met geïntegreerde stoffen

18 · 6 juni 2002 · intermediair 23

Storia, passioni e futuro di Droog Design, gruppo olandese votato alla rigorosa asciuttezza concettuale

The history, passions and future of Droog Design, Dutch group devoted to lean, dry design

PIERLUIGI SERRI

Droog Design Superfluo

new

new

LESS + MORE

droog

Ottagono, July/August 2002

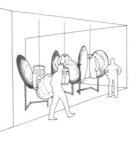

Window drops A new collaboration between Levi's RED and Droog results in a window concept composed of self-adhesive PVC drops. The design is developed during a brainstorm session on the subject of glass. Participants are Levi's fashion designers and two product designers invited by Droog: Arnout Visser and Bas van Tol. Together they delve deep into the qualities of glass.

Newsletter Droog Now,
October 2002, design alone

DROOG NOW

No. 7, October 2002, € 1.00

Real Life Revisited	The Product Matters	**INSIDE**
hotel droog ★ page 2	Levi's Red® not on page 2	droog blue coloured edition

UPDATE

New and better place!

Shop and exhibition space

1 human= 1 human= 1 human=
1 human= 1 human= 1 human=
1 human= 1 human= 1 human=
1 human= 1 human= 1 human=

Masters

Re-inventing Rituals

Redemption of the fake

DROOG N

No. 7, October 2002, € 1.00

Real Life Revisited	The Product Matters
hotel droog ★ page 2	Levi's Red® not on page 2

UPDATE

New and better place!

Shop and exhibition space

AMSTERDAM: Up until a few months ago Droog Design had a formal office in a quiet street. It simply did not match

1 human= 1 human=
1 human= 1 human=
1 human= 1 human=
1 human= 1 human=

Droog Design for Valli & Valli The Italian manufacturer of door handles Valli & Valli commissions Droog to develop a new series of door handles. The first one is by Ronald Lewerissa, of the Dutch studio Flex Development. It calls upon the manifestation of the method of production and the choice of material. The door handle is carried out straightforwardly: concept dictates design. The laser technique used for the metal door handle reduces the number of parts to a minimum and additionally allows applying logo's or other information to the handle. The handle named Anapurna is first shown in Milan and is now being produced by Valli & Valli.

Less & More
A new publication by Renny Ramakers on Droog Design against the background of current material culture Less + More - Droog Design in Context is published.
Design Thonik

change of address

droog design®

Rusland 3
1012 CK Amsterdam
the Netherlands

t + 31 20 6269809
f + 31 20 6388828
info@droogdesign.nl
www.droogdesign.nl

former address;
Sarphatikade 11, 1017 WV Amsterdam, the Netherlands

Droog & Co. During the April Furniture Fair in Milan Droog introduces a new activity.
It starts a Droog shop, designed by Richard Hutten. The reason is the continious
complaint that Droog products are not for sale in regular shops. This sales activity
is also a prelude to the new space Droog is to open in May in Amsterdam.
Up until now Droog Design has had an office in a quiet street in Amsterdam. It turns
out that visitors expect to be able to see and buy things. Apart from that, Droog has
the feeling that they are not understood well enough in the Netherlands. So they seek
to strengthen their roots in Dutch culture and work on a more accessible location
where Droog products can be seen and purchased and that also allows exhibitions
with the occasional opening.
So Droog Design opens Droog & Co., a small exhibition space right in the centre
of Amsterdam. It is a place with centuries old history, completely restored by the
Amsterdam municipality.
During the year Droog & Co. presents a compilation of Hotel droog, designed by
Richard Hutten, together with the videowork Hotel droog by Fendry Ekel, a follow-up
of Franck Bragigand's painting act in Milan, to be concluded by an auction of the
painted objects, the work of graduates from the Masters at the Design Academy in
Eindhoven and the state service Tableau Vivant designed by Marcel Wanders for the
Alsace prefecture.

Brutus, January 8, 2002

アムスの新名所!? 〈ドローグ・ショップ〉の開店です。

The Product Matters

DMD is taken over by the company The Product Matters (TPM), based in Amsterdam. The company's strategy is to establish Droog as a consumer brand and to spread Droog products in shops all over the world.

Auction and exhibition /
human = human,
Franck Bragigand

IM-Masters The first batch of students of the IM-Masters course at the Design Academy, Eindhoven graduate. Cynthia Hathaway from Canada has studied the strange borderline between the fake and the real. An important part of this project is a series of photographs she made in the miniature city of Madurodam in The Hague, from a position as if she were a resident photographer. In strange pictures fake miniature perfection gives in to the reality of life-sized decay. Michelle Huang from Singapore has studied the way in which cultures mix by observing Chinese people that live and 'acculturize' in the Netherlands. She notices that for the young generations living in Amsterdam the old rituals are not as obvious as they are for Chinese brought up in their country of origin. Huang is interested in the way in which the host culture and future generations of Chinese can build a new framework together. So she decides to develop tableware to reinvent rituals. A bowl with a handle emphasizes the ritual of eating rice with the bowl in your hand. She also designs a bowl with an extra pocket to leave some food, because if a guest in China eats everything, this is an indication that there was not enough.

**Exhibition / Re inventing rituals,
Michelle Huang**

Tableau Vivant The Alsace Prefecture needed a new set of tableware for official occasions and commissions Droog Design to find a designer. Marcel Wanders is asked for the job. The starting point for his design is the famous French slogan 'Freedom, Equality, Brotherhood'. It results in a table setting in which all the individual objects play a role in connection with others, a so called living table. The plates and bowls are made of porcelain. The chandeliers and vases are made of original slender Alsacian wine bottles, plated with silver. Before the tableware is handed over to the prefect, it is shown at Droog & Co. in Amsterdam.

House and Home Abitare il Tempo, a fair in
Verona features a special exhibition on
'Living in the 21st century'. Massimo Morozzi,
Alessandro Mendini, Denis Santachiara, Droog
Design and two other participants are all allo-
cated 200 m2 to show their vision on the current
home. Droog Design presents 'House & Home',
referring to a so-called united Europe which
in fact is a pattern of identities, expressed by
integrating regional clichés in products.
Design studio Traast & Gruson is asked to make
an installation for this presentation. The house
they design is decorated with a range of Droog
products selected according to their capability
to carry some subdued national sign.
For instance Tejo Remy's rag chair is especially
made in a version to include a Scottish rag.

Shopping for Terence Conran Every year Terence Conran, the founder of the Design Museum in London, allows a famous designer to shop for 50.000 euro worth of products of his or her choice that consequently are turned into an exhibition and added to the collection of the Conran Foundation afterwards. This year Gijs Bakker and Renny Ramakers of Droog Design are asked. They decide to make strictly separate lists of favourite products. They discover that their choices have only three objects in common. Among the pieces chosen by Ramakers is a 1988 Afghan carpet that, true to local tradition, is woven with symbols from daily life, but instead of birds and vases, it is emblazoned with Soviet guns and helicopters. She also chooses a silver French fries fork designed by Sophie Lachaert. Her comment: 'Sophie Lachaert is Belgian and in Belgium you find the best French fries in the world. It's worth eating them with a silver fork.' A remarkable product chosen by Bakker is the bling bling, designed by Frank Tjepkema, a golden necklace with a cross compiled of logos. Gijs Bakker's comment: 'worshipping logos all crucified together'. He also picks the birthday calendar by Richard Hutten. Both Gijs and Renny choose a poster waste bin by Jos van der Meulen.

Exhibition / Gijs and Renny go shopping, Design museum London

Design installation, Mylene Jonker

2003

Presentation Milan, April 9-14

Your Choice

Concrete Architectural Associates, Cecilie Frostad Egeberg, Simon Heijdens, Onkar Singh Kular, Claudia Linders, NEXT Architects, Ted Noten, Vincent de Rijk, Frederik Roijé, Maartje Steenkamp, Thonik, Frank Tjepkema, United Statements

+

Play-back

Markus Bader, Sebastian Oschatz, Max Wolf

+

And...

Simon Heijdens, Michelle Huang, Matijs Korpershoek, Susanne Philippson, Paolo Ulian, Marcel Wanders

Your Choice The project Your Choice, first shown during the International Furniture Fair in Milan, shows how cultural and commercial imperatives can be combined. For the first time Droog Design integrates sales with a critical presentation. This is done very consciously because the selling aspect is part of the concept. Droog expects some action from visitors.

The title of this exhibition Your Choice refers to the title of one chapter of Naomi Klein's book No Logo, called No Choice. The exhibition is mainly intended to provoke questions on the choices we make in relation to the phenomenon of branding, born from curiosity about visitor's behaviour. Obvious considerations are blown up or turned upside down.

The installation, designed by Concrete Architectural Associates, consists of over ten thousand bottles of specially bottled 'droog' water. Visitors are invited to dismantle the exhibition by buying a bottle for 1 euro. So during the show one can witness the installation change. It may sound like a paradox: challenging brands and at the same time branding the droog label according to usual merchandising conventions. But it is all part of the concept. People can choose for themselves whether they want to participate in the game.

What happens for instance when 50 identical felt bags are offered, each with a different price from 1 to 50 euros? Would the cheapest be sold first? Or do other motives play a role, making someone grab a more expensive one? The products are all the same, at least if the prominent price tags are removed. Whoever chooses to leave it also unveils something about his or her spending pattern.

The majority of visitors choose cheap. The bags priced from 1 to 10 euros are sold immediately and after that it goes up slowly. Only a few people dare to buy a more expensive bag. Some even try to cheat by exchanging tags.

Are people willing to pay more for a T-shirt bearing texts like 'out of fashion'? And is this enhanced by adding the brand droog to it? A product normally regarded as inferior can indeed be made more expensive and yet still be sold because it is deliberately mentioned on the product.

Your Choice also points at branding. Claudia Linders asks visitors to remove the so cherished logo from their design clothing and replace it with an 'Unlabeled' tag. She needs 1700 names in order to make a label dress out of them, a piece of shared identities. It turns out that the visitors most eager to remove the labels from their clothing are dressed in low-image clothing. People who are really wearing high-end brands sometimes refuse to cut off the labels.

T-shirts marked up in price

Simon Heijdens, United
Statements
2003

Set of bowls

Vincent de Rijk
2003
ceramics, glazed on
the inside
various sizes

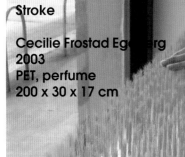

Stroke

Cecilie Frostad Egenberg
2003
PET, perfume
200 x 30 x 17 cm

100 Brooches

Ted Noten
2003
different pieces of a red
Mercedes Benz
various sizes
limited, numbered edition of 100
brooches for Droog Design

The Norwegian Queen expresses her interest in design with 'Stoke', the perfume dispenser from Cecilia Frostad Egeberg, that was presented by droog during the Salone 2003.

your choice
det är ditt val

Du är välkommen att delta i det här projektet:

· Du bidrar till nedmonteringen av utställningen genom att köpa en flaska droog-vatten (10 kr).*

· Väga göra dig av med din Prada- Chanel- eller den varumärkesetikett du nu bär.
Ge den till oss så för du i i utbyte etiketten UNILABELED.

· Spela dataspelet och ta reda på vem du är.

· Rör försiktigt vid "gräset" och skapa din egen doft.

· Du kan köpa en, av flera, identiskt lika väskor, efter ditt eget val.*

· Du kan välja T-shirts som gått upp i pris när du egentligen väntat dig ett rabatterat pris (baspris 100 kr).*

· Du kan beställa en vas tillverkad efter din egen namnteckning (29 000 kr).*

· Du kan få din egen bärbara del ihân en Mercedes Benz (upplaga 100; 1 300 kr styck).*

· Om du gillar numrerade sockerbitar så hittar du dem här (upplaga 12; 1 100 kr per box).*

· Du kan välja mellan 54 olika storlekar på en skal och får därigenom en unik produkt med många användningsområden.*

· Välj mellan 3 utställningskataloger som är olika och ändå lika på samma gång (upplaga 1000; 75 kr styck).*

* Alla slutgiltiga transaktioner görs vid disken.

The presentation Your Choice is a big success. After Milan it goes to Rotterdam, Stockholm and Prague.

Play Back The project Play Back by Max Wolf, Markus Bader and Sebastian Oschatz integrates modern technology in our familiar surrounding. Masterpieces from the past are brought to the height of modern technology. For instance, an original TECHNICS DJ's turntable from 1980 is adapted to play mp3 music recordings from a chip and a mp3 server.

Day Tripper, Streetscape Furniture, Mori Building Company Tokyo Roppongi Hills
in Tokyo, one of the largest private building developer in Japan opens in May.
11 hectares space provides Tokyo with a Cultural Centre, complete with an art
museum, hotel, cinema restaurants, offices and residential towers.
Droog Design is one of the eleven designers and architects, among them Jasper
Morrison, Ettore Sottsass, Toyo Ito, Andrea Branzi and Ron Arad, who are invited
to develop street furniture for the area. Droog Design gets a strip of 7 by 1.25 m
to work on.
Droog asks Jurgen Bey for this commission. The designer allows himself to be inspired
by the different postures people assume on the street. He takes pictures and observes
how they move during the day. Next he selects human silhouettes and arranges them
to form a natural order in time. Computer morphing from one position to the next over
the available seven metres produces the basic bench shape. After that Bey adds the
shapes of old furniture. The bench, called Day Tripper, is made of Polyurethane foam
covered with glass reinforced Polyester with a silk screen flower pattern.

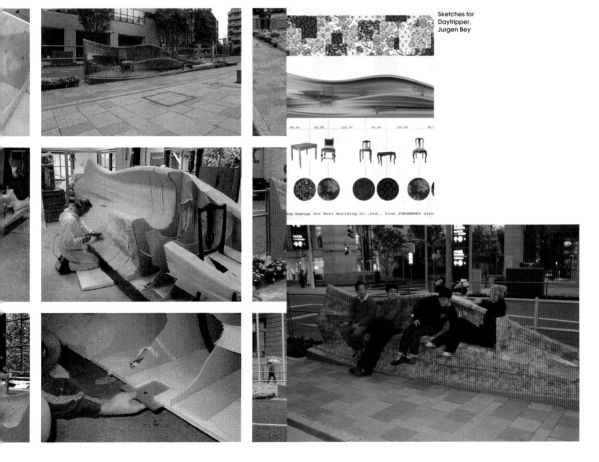

Sketches for
Daytripper,
Jurgen Bey

Gollandskaya Komnata, St. Petersburg To celebrate the 300th anniversary of he city of St. Petersburg in 2003, the Netherlands organize a week of Dutch Culture'. Various Dutch theatre and dance performances are presented in various theatres in the Russian city. The Premsela Foundation for Dutch design asks Droog to furnish a small coffee shop in the Baltic House Theatre. This commission has to be carried out within a period of two months.

At the forefront of Droog's concept is the wish to re-use the existing situation as much as possible and, given the location in a theatre, to achieve a theatrical effect. Franck Bragigand is asked to paint the space from top to bottom. He makes a colour scheme of different shades of green. Droog requests Jurgen Bey to apply his streetscape project to single chairs. Antique chairs are covered with layers of glass fibre, the final layer having an integrated flower pattern. Connie Groenewegen bases her designs for the waiter's uniforms on second hand clothing. The result is a combination of domesticity and theatre that plays with historical styles in a contemporary manner. A wink as it were to the imperial rooms in the Hermitage.

Droog meets Bless Once again, Jean Pierre Blanc, curator of events in the Villa Noailles in Hyères, France, asks Droog Design to do a project with Bless, a small fashion company established by fashion designers Desiree Heiss and Inez Kaag. It resides both in Paris and Berlin. Droog and Bless decide that they themselves and Bless are to react to five of each other's designs. On behalf of Droog, designer Connie Groenewegen will deal with the products of Bless. Her main observation is that Bless tends to cover objects in such a way that they neutralize their image and sometimes take away their original function. Groenewegen buys a couple of old seats and covers them with unbleached cotton. To compensate for the neutralizing effect of the white layer and at the same time adding a new layer with communicative properties, she drapes envelopes of silk on the seats. Embroidered with human portraits, they can also serve to cover the persons sitting on the seats.

Bless reacts to Droog Design likewise, except that they do it very subtly by adding 'placemats' to five separate objects. Marcel Wander's birdfeeder for instance gets a mat consisting of a bird food spiral.

The Droog Design books are put in a bookcase with the backs inside. For recognition they get long ribbons stuck to their backs with the titles written on them. They hang from the shelves. Specially for the exhibition Droog and Bless design a Bless Droog T-shirt. It is decorated with a Bless logo on one side and a Droog one on the other that are stitched through both layers of the T-shirt. Wearing the T-shirt implies making a choice between slipping the arm either over or under the stitching.

droog / BLESS shirt

Droog Bless
Droog Bless

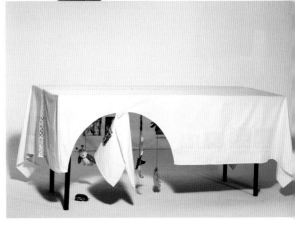

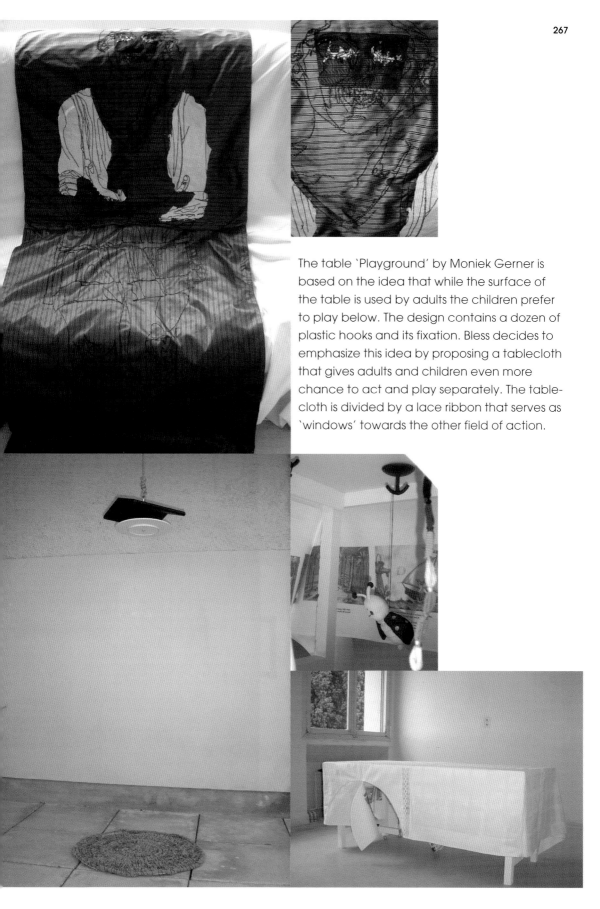

The table 'Playground' by Moniek Gerner is based on the idea that while the surface of the table is used by adults the children prefer to play below. The design contains a dozen of plastic hooks and its fixation. Bless decides to emphasize this idea by proposing a tablecloth that gives adults and children even more chance to act and play separately. The tablecloth is divided by a lace ribbon that serves as 'windows' towards the other field of action.

New masters The 3i-Masters course programme at the Design Academy Eindhoven, now called IM-Masters, takes a new direction.

From September the three courses named industrial, interior and identity, which before were led by three different organizations, are connected in one programme. Droog Design is asked to become the head of the IM-Masters programme. In the new programme research is the starting point for all designing activities. The students work on two projects per six months. The teachers switch each semester.

TPM bankrupt In May 2003 the bad news arrives that The Product Matters (TPM) has filed for bankruptcy. Fortunately Droog Design finds an investor who wants to invest in development, production and distribution under the name droog. This organisation is operating independent from the Droog foundation but is carefully supervised by Droog Design. One of the main targets is to improve quality, to set up wider circulation and to offer products at lower prices.

Masters graduation Two of the most interesting IM-Masters graduation projects of the Design Academy in Eindhoven are by Stuart Sproule from Canada and Praoranuj Siridej from Thailand. Stuart Sproule, a fanatic skater, studies the physical relationship between man and urban space. He investigates the opportunities of what he calls urban body space. He pictures the following scenario: an elegant girl with a fashion-able handbag takes the elevator to the tenth floor of a high-rise building. There she unfolds her bag that appears to consist of a thin high tech cable, climbs through the window and looses herself in a spectacular ride down along the façade. Another proposition by Sproule is a swing that is part of a garment. When you see a particularly challenging bridge you can instantly use it to enjoy yourself.

The difference with the project by Praoranuj Siridej couldn't be bigger. She promotes the qualities of being old: Seniors are wiser, can concentrate better, are able to listen and they are slower, in the positive sense of the word. She seeks cooperation with a club of elderly people and together with them she presents a restaurant in which everything is done with wisdom and care.

Nodesign
Nostyle
Droog Design
네덜란드 디자인그룹 드록디자인 展

초청강연회 자료집
예술의전당 한가람디자인미술관

No style no design Kim Sang Kyu, curator of
The Hangaram Art Museum in Seoul takes the
initiative to organize a major exhibition on Droog
Design. The museum presents 65 products from
the Droog Collection occupying a space of
800m2. This makes the museum the first venue
to show an overview of 10 years Droog Design.
At this occasion the book ‘Less + More’ by Renny
Ramakers is published in Korean.

BOOK 01

〈드록 디자인 1991-1996〉

글 Ids van Zijl · 사진 Maurice Boyer · 편집/디자인 Studio Gonnissen en Widdershoven ·
Amsterdam Centraal Museum, Utrecht 1997 · 133페이지 · 판형 17.5x24.5(cm)

하드 커버의 책 표지에서 보이듯 흑백사진 속의 젊은 남녀 한 쌍이 밝은 표정으로 오르를 올리고 있는 사진이다. 그들은 새 의자인 아래로 의자나 장롱이나 하는 세간들을 들이고 있는 중이다. 책을 몇 장 넘기면서 옷들을 벗어제낀 남자가 열심히 벽면의 한 쪽 기슭을 떼고 있다. 그 옆엔 드록의 디자이너 리차드 휴튼(Richard Hutten)의 학상김용 의자 십자가 (the Cross)가 놓여져 있다. 읽든(보든) 이는 책장을 넘기면서 드록의 디자인 사용·초안들에서 커튼, 목욕탕 바닥에들에서 서랍장에 이르기까지 많은 곳곳에 의자들을 펼쳐놓고 자리매기 하는 모습을 관찰할 수 있다. 책의 서문에서 저자는 다음과 같이 밝히고 있다.

"1990년대부터 드록디자인은 세계 디자인계를 가로지르면 무성한 인상을 자아내면서 오고 있다. 그러나 드록의 대부를 지키면 저지 않은 사람들이, 한 철의 유행이 그러하듯 언젠가는 급속히 퇴색될 것이라는나 그게 아니라도 그게 서서히 사라지게 될 것이라는나 수근대곤 했었다. 물론 드록이 앞으로도 계속 발전될 것이라고 생각한 사람도 있었다. 드록의 축척된 부산에 대한 채무로, 힌 정의를 미쳐 내리기도 전에 나온 유트레흐트 중앙 미술관(Utrecht's Centraal Museum)이 드록의 디자인물을 소장하게 결정한 것이라만.

이를 가능케 한 드록의 참립자나 디자이너들이나 작업 동기와 그게 대한 의견, 배경 등에 관한 이해를 수집하는 것은 사뭇 중요하게 여겨진다. 이 책의 내용을 읽기 위해, 이 책은 디자인들과 그림과 디자이너들을 포함하여 드록의 디자이너들에게는 다음과 같은 질문들이 던져졌다.

당신은 누구인가? / 당신의 배경은 무엇인가? / 드록 디자인 컬렉션에 포함된 당신의 디자인은 어떤 것인가? / 그것들의 제작동기는 무엇인가? / 당신은 요즘 어떤 일을 하고 있는가? / 그래서도 언제까지 일하고 있는가? / 드록의 디자인들을 통 취고만 무엇인가? / 당신의 작업은 제작하고 드록 디자인의 당신에게 어떤 의미를 갖는가? / 그것이 얼마나 중요한 것이 드록으로 인해 어떤 변화가 생긴 것 같든가 생각해본가? (중략)

서문의 내용을 통해 알 수 있든, 이 책은 프로젝트, 중앙 미술관(Utrecht's Centraal Museum)의 컬렉션에 추가된 1991년부터 1996년까지의 드록 디자인 200개 작업들을, 그림들의 작업과 그 간단한 약력, 드록 디자인에 참여하게 된 동기 등과 함께 보여주는 흑백 카탈로그 개념의 사진책이다. 세 집에 이사오는 젊은 커플의 살림살이 육에 걸들어진 드록의 디자인 사물들, 이 책은 그것들이 일상의 모습들에서 얼마나 제 몫을 가능히도 매끈하게 어떤지, 이 물건들을 이로 할 수 있다 라는 식의 예시들이다.

비저만 드록에 추구하고 있는 혁명적 의미에 대한 주제나게 참신이 때문 자나처, 디자인에 본질을 끝은 이들이 그것이 실제하는 것이나고 그대로 버려지지 않는에 관한 저자의 객관적인 성질에 대해 묵인에 마구심성을 자아내기도 한다. 더욱이 그러한 찬사들은, 드록 디자인에 작업 살펴보면 그 실체로서 그 실효화를 상상 확인해보 되는 입장에게서만 다는 낯설 수도 있겠다.

마지막으로 편집/디자인에 관한 이야기가 하나면 다, 시원시원한 프리징의 사물이고 사물이고 잘 꽉 책은 흑백사진들은 어제의 앨을 아는 깨금한 그리드 시스템, 산 세리프 글꼴들과 어불러 네덜란드 복 디자인 특유의 느낌을 잘 전해준다.

Designnet Seoul, May 2003

Exhibition / Kyozon Gallery, Tokyo, October 9-12

예술의전당
한가람디자인미술관
2003.9.26-10.19

개막식
9.25(목) 오후 5시
디자인미술관 로비

워크샵
9.25(목) 오전 10시-오후 4시
디자인미술관 세미나실

강연회
9.26(금) 오후 1시-4시
예술의전당 서예박물관 4층 대회의실

Het Parool, February 28, 2003

ERWAN & RONAN BOUROULLEC

Ceci n'est pas un toilettafel

Ze zijn ook Frans. En daardoor zal het wel komen dat ze steeds met Philippe Starck worden vergeleken, zeggen ze. Voor de broers Bouroullec geen dikdoenerij. Ze waren even hier voor de opening van hun expositie in de galerie van Droog Design. 'We ontwerpen het liefst zo veel mogelijk tegelijkertijd.' EMILIE ESCHER

Stoel

Vaas

Vaasje FOTO'S CARO BONINK

W aar ze allemaal geweest zijn, weten ze niet meer. Maar het was een wilde nacht voor de broers Bouroullec, voor ze voor het eerst in Amsterdam, Lijkbleek komen ze Galerie Droog Design binnen. Anderhalf uur later dan eigenlijk afgesproken. "Wil je de officiële of onofficiële versie?" lacht Ronan (31). Hij is de grapjes van de twee. Zijn vijf jaar jongere broer Erwan is een stuk serieuzer. Liever wil Erwan niet bij de tentoongestelde voorwerpen praten, maar in het kantoorgedeelte van de galerie, bij is bang dat het interview beïnvloed zal verstoren. "Ik zit liever aan die tafel daar."

De broers Bouroullec zijn hard op weg naar grote faam. Ze hebben een uitgebreide tentoonstelling in het Londonse Design Museum gehad, werden door de Salon du Meuble in Parijs uitgeroepen tot ontwerpers van 2003, en heetten in menig artikel 'de opvolgers van Philippe Starck'. Dat aan best een last kunnen zijn, maar de broers gaan er niet onder gebukt. "Ach, zo noemen ze een ander maar omdat we ook Frans zijn, denk ik," zegt Erwan die het woord doet, omdat zijn Engels volgens broer Ronan beter is. Ze zijn ook niet onder de indruk van de naam Starck. "We konden stage bij hem lopen, maar wilden liever op eigen kracht wat bereiken. Nu zijn we daar ook trots op." Het is een foute, bescheiden tentoonstelling die de broers in Droog Design houden. "Zie het als een voorportaal van ons werk," zegt Erwan. Meest in het oog springend is de zwarte, een beeldbuisachtige vaas met een orchidee erin. Nee, ze willen er niet mee verkoudgaan dat je beter naar bloemen kan kijken dan naar de zin. "Wij kijken graag zo"

Er staan nog meer obscure vazen. Je kunt er een bloem in steken en water in gieten. Maar daarmee houdt de vergelijking met de doorsnee vaas ook op, vooral bij dat ene geval op het eveneens door hen ontworpen kleed. Ben bestekreikje voor in de afwasmachine, misschien. Maar een vaas? De toilettafel daarentegen, die voor ons, de twee aanwezige vrouwen, toch duidelijk en toiletafel is, blijkt helemaal geen toilettafel te zijn, maar gewoon een tafel die tegen de muur kan staan. Kortom: het Bouroullec-design laat zich niet zo snel duiden.

Erwan: "Onze voorwerpen laten zich niet zo snel uitleggen, nee. Je kunt niet zo snel zeggen: dit is dit en dat kan je ermee doen. We geven nooit zo duidelijk een identiteit aan een ding. We vinden het leuker als mensen self maar zien wat het is en hoe ze het gebruiken."

Typisch voorbeeld van een ander onduidbaar object is hun kast - niet in Droog Design te zien - die meer weg heeft van een groot, grillig rezenwijnrek. "Het is heel licht, van piepschuim, makkelijk verplaatsbaar en je kunt het ook prima gebruiken om een soort afscheiding te maken in een kantoor. Het blijft transparant in een ruimte."

De twee broers zijn niet heel veel ontwerpen tegelijkertijd bezig. Een horlogeverpakking voor Issey Miyake, kantoormeubilair voor Vitra, juwelen. "Nee, het wordt niet te veel," zeggen beiden eerlijg. Erwan: "Voor ons is het juist belangrijk met zo veel mogelijk tegelijkertijd bezig te zijn. Je blijft je beter bewust van de complexiteit van alles. Er is bijna niets wat ik niet zou willen ontwerpen."

Ronan: "Een geweer niet. Wapens niet."

Erwan: "En hoe onbekender het voor ons is, hoe beter. We proberen er onbevangen tegenaan te kijken. Neem een auto. Voor ons is het uiterlijk van een gewone auto niet vanzelfsprekend. Wij zouden eerder proberen een ander soort auto te maken. Wat voor soort auto, daar kan ik je nu geen antwoord op geven. Het hangt van het proces af, en dat kan voortdurend veranderen. Je tekent, stelt bij, vraagt je af wat je ermee kunt doen en als je pech hebt, begin je weer van voren af aan." Dat gebeurde met de fruitschaal die in Droog Design

staat. "We waren een half jaar bezig geweest met het ontwikkelen van het materiaal. Gaat het in de oven helemaal kapot. We konden wel huilen."

Elk ding wordt van begin tot einde samen ontworpen. Het is niet zo dat Ronan het horloge doet en Erwan de auto. Erwan: "Hij tekent wat, ik zeg wat bij. We praten er weer over. Zo gaat het." Het eerste dat ze samen ontwierpen, dat weten ze zelf eens niet meer. Want wanneer begon het echt, het is een complexe vraag. Het ging vanzelf, Ronan: "Het begon al toen we hutten maakten samen."

En ruzie? Hebben ze ooit ruzie? En of, Ronan: "Pff, soms scheldt het niet veel of we vechten elkaar de tent uit. Maar ik denk dat iedereen die zo lang en nauw samenwerkt ruzie krijgt. Het voordeel is dat wij alles tegen elkaar kunnen roepen en dat het daarna weer over is. Het werkt alleen maar goed."

Het werk van Erwan en Ronan Bouroullec is nog tot en met 22 maart in Droog Design te bezichtigen, Rusland 3.

Erwan & Ronan Bouroullec

Droog & Co. Droog & Co presents the first exhibition of the French brothers Bouroullec in the Netherlands, an overview of the Placebo project by British designers Dunne and Raby and the results of the project that Droog and Bless did together in Hyères.

droog

Exhibition / Dunne + Raby, The Placebo Project at Droog & Co

THE PLACEBO EFFECT

MARK RAPPOLT INVESTIGATES HOW DUNNE + RABY'S PLACEBO PRODUCTS
ARE FURTHERING THE FUTURE OF DESIGN

Designing the Invisible
Dunne & Raby
The Placebo Project

New address After one and half years the location at Rusland 3 in Amsterdam appears to be short of space for all Droog Design activities. In the beginning of 2004 Droog Design will move to a 700m2 space in another historical building in the centre of Amsterdam. The new location at Staalstraat 7 partly dates from 1641. It used to be the space in which Rembrandt has painted his famous painting The Syndics of the Clothmakers' Guild. The public space on the ground floor will be designed by Bas van Tol. The office spaces on the upper floors will be painted by Franck Bragigand. These new premises have enough space for a permanent exhibition of the Droog Collection, changing exhibitions of Dutch and international design, documentation, an artist in residence and of course the Droog Design office. There will also be informal meetings where designers can have interdisciplinary discussions on fixed themes.

below: The Droog team, December 2003

Hein Schutte, Renny Ramakers, Mariëlle de Vooys, Gijs Bakker, Astrid Honold and Nora Schuit.

Some of Droog's interns from 2002 to 2004:

Marije Veenstra, Thijs Ewalts, Anouk Kef, Linde Dorenbosch and Mylène Jonker.

2004

Presentation Milan, April 14–18

Go Slow
Installation: Sloom, Rianne Makkink,
Herman Verkerk in co-operation with Hansje
van Halem, Frau Hanke (graphic design),
Kees Wijker, Bregje de Heer, carpenter 't Woud
(construction), Praoranuj Siridej (concept
Senior Service)
Slow Food: Saai Design, Marije Vogelzang
Products: Jurgen Bey, Chris Kabel, MIKAN,
Saai Design, Tadaaki Narita, NEXT Architects
and Aura Luz Melis, Noriko Yasuda

GO SLOW
SLOW INVITATION
SLOW PRESENTATION
SLOW SERVICE
SLOW EXPERIENCE

DROOG DESIGN
during Salone del Mobile
La Galleria Postart
MILANO
April 14th - 18th, 2004

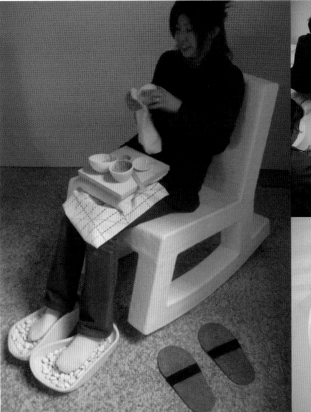

A moment of peace
amidst all the busyness
during the furniture fair.

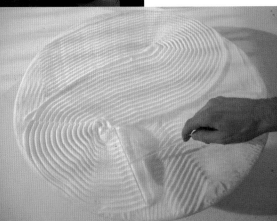

Droog's 12th presentation in Milan is based on the concept of Go Slow. Slowness has become a rare quality in our modern, urban world which is dominated by speed and instant consumption. Slowness is a luxury.

In a white environment Droog offers visitors a moment of peace amidst all the busyness during the furniture fair. Senior citizens serve a snack and a drink attentively and in their own tempo. The menus are embroidered. Oranges are pressed by hand and the teabags are folded on the spot and sewn together with a few stitches. Visitors entering the space can choose a snack and a drink, pay the cashier and receive a beautiful serviette. Maybe they have to wait a moment. When their turn comes they have to don large, felt slippers which force you to walk slowly and at the same time polish the floor. You can take a chair from the wall or relax in a rocking chair with your feet in the Footrest, designed by Noriko Yasuda, for a foot massage. There are long tables filled with salt, which you can sit at and rake over like Zen gardens. Slowing down also offers room for social interaction. The senior servants become so absorbed in their role that they spontaneously begin to massage visitors or sing them an old Dutch song. In the meantime the lamps gradually become brighter and warmer. When the staff arrives with a warm cloth it is time to leave. The visitors may take the dirty cups with them in their serviette.

Go Slow in Rotterdam and London

After the Salone del Mobile in Milan, the Go Slow presentation is also featured in the Rotterdam Kunsthal during the Kunsthal Food Festival. The Victoria & Albert Museum in London presents Go Slow during Friday Late Night 'Consume this!', an evening about sustainable consumption in fashion, design and gastronomy. Go Slow London focuses on the DVD that Fendry Ekel made of Go Slow Milan. Special tea is made from Drente leaves and biscuits from forgotten grain. These are served by two of the senior citizens who had also worked in Milan and the Kunsthal, together with four English ladies aged over eighty years. The visitors use the same serviettes and are offered tea and biscuits in the same cups and saucers on the same tray with holes as in Milan. Afterwards, some visitors say that they felt as though they were participating in the video.

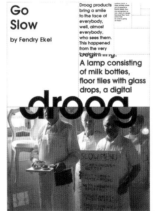

Go Slow
by Fendry Ekel

Droog products bring a smile to the face of everybody, well, almost everybody, who sees them. This happened from the very beginning. A lamp consisting of milk bottles, floor tiles with glass drops, a digital

Some of the few remaining senior citizens who still know how to manually peel shrimps came over especially for the Go Slow presentation in Rotterdam.

デザインを鍵に、「今」を体感する5日間。

ドローグ×つみきでスローなカフェ誕生。　　　Droog Design "Go Slow"

droog

ミラノ・サローネでも、
人気のカフェがTDBに。

Go Slow Tokyo

In Tokyo, visitors to Go Slow can enjoy an experience in a Tsumiki House which has been built specially for the presentation. It turns out that a pallet of products has not arrived. What are mainly lacking are the slippers and Fatlamps. But a visit to the Tokyo Hands do-it-yourself store makes up for everything. With the aid of felt, paper and existing light fittings, new slippers and lamps are conjured forth in the wink of an eye. The little building survives an earthquake of 5.7 on the Richter scale, and is then threatened by an imminent typhoon, which results in the presentation having to be taken down. The next morning everything is built up again and the visitors to Go Slow are quietly received by Japanese senior citizens. Mina Wu has designed aprons for the presentation and a virtual alarm clock by Itay Noy, which runs more slowly, is specially employed for the occasion.

DROOG EVENT 1
Open Borders

Presentation Lille European Cultural Capital, September 4 – November 28

With the project Open Borders, Droog Design launches the first edition of the three-yearly DROOG EVENT. The aim of this event is to illustrate every three years the latest developments of European design as well as the links between design and other disciplines, such as the visual arts and architecture. The spirit in which the event is conceived as well as the presented projects illustrate a common attitude. The idea is to contribute to international debate and make the latest developments more accessible to the general public.

Open Borders

The first edition of DROOG EVENT, entitled Open Borders, is presented within the context of Lille 2004, European Capital of Culture. Almost 85 projects by artists, designers and architects are presented, and others dealing with (artificial) nature, social prosperity and the open source movement, which consists in the creator and user dipping freely into diverse sources. Open Borders does not question the boundaries between the disciplines, but considers them as a fait accompli or a finished debate.

The latest technological developments and social movements have inspired a multitude of concepts in the world of design, art and architecture. Sampling, hacking and mixing, intrinsic values in the digital world, are all echoed in the creative spheres.
Architects, artists, designers and creatives from other disciplines interpret, handle, simulate,

reproduce and appropriate original works. They use each available product, concept and system. They combine cultures, introduce new techniques into the heart of old products and play around with author's rights. They work commercial brands and systems.

The consumer is invited to participate in this process. One of the works on show is Tord Boontje's Rough and Ready chair, based on a drawing which he sends all over the world, so that everyone can make the chair themselves. Dick van Hoff shows a wallpapering machine with which everyone can make their own wallpaper. The designer no longer completely controls the implementation of the projects.

Nature also participates and opens the way. The lifespan of the lamps by English designer Paul Cocksedge depends on the life of a flower. The buildings by French architect Edouard François are 'swallowed up' by nature. Front, the Swedish design studio, allows rats and insects to intervene in their projects. At the same time, nature is copied, manipulated and controlled. Robots chirp like birds in the trees, butterfly wings are coloured with fresh motifs. Trees are placed at the top of pillars and rabbits can be seen with embroidered ears.

Enjoying a massage by the Tickle Salon by Maria Verstappen and Erwin Driessens

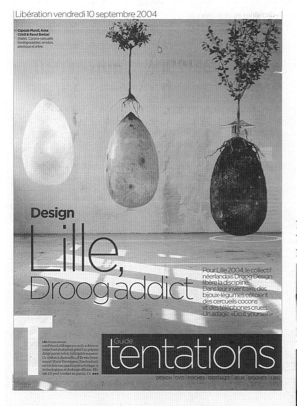

This evolution leads to a reinterpretation of ideas and products that are of no value or have been abandoned. Used products and forgotten shapes are recuperated and former techniques are the object of new attention. Shirts are transformed into wedding dresses. A bent gate becomes a bench. The exhibition shows that artists, architects and designers seek to re-establish links uniting human beings and nature. They express a need to do more with less, to question the social system. Old paper is re-used in typographical creation. A Coca-Cola crate is transformed into a lamp. In this hybrid and virtual world, the loss of contact with reality becomes a source of inspiration.

NICHE/DROOG EVENTS

LILLE DROOG SEASON IS STILL CAPITAL

While drawing towards the end of its year as European Capital of Culture, Lille is far from slowing down. Highlight of Season 3, which began last month, is Droog Events, a specially commissioned exhibition of large-scale projects about the city.

Design Etc, Open Borders, an exhibition of 80 projects from young designers and artists working in Europe in the Tri Postal Building, is the focus of Droog's interventions in Lille. The exhibits, in the Droog tradition, are all examples of the 'pen source' movement of design that endorses recycling old products into new, and allows users to participate in the designs themselves – perhaps making their own.

Marti Guixé's 'motorway tape', which enables children to build their own highways at home, is shown next to Dick Von Hoff's wallpaper machine, and lights by Paul Cocksedge depend on the life of a flower. Droog's philosophy is largely concerned with the need to do more with less, and to provide concepts that put the social status quo up for discussion.

Droog has also organised residencies by young designers around Lille in factories, shops, and La Braderie (a citywide, single-day, bring-and-buy sale). Designers are invited to radically redesign items brought along by visitors.

At the Musée de l'Hospice Comtesse is Strangely Familiar: Design and Everyday Life, an exhibition of designs and architecture that reference and/or transform commonplace objects and conditions, including Martin Ruiz de Azua's Basic House, a pocket-sized inflatable shelter, and Tumble House, a six-sided building designed by Koers, Zeinstra, and van Gelderen of the Netherlands which, when rotated into different positions, changes the functionality of elements; for example, a door becomes a window.

Also being installed over one of the city's main streets for this third term are 30m-high arches, by Australian artist team Bambuco.

Freshen Up

Part of Open Borders is a workshop by Connie Groenewegen, Arnout Visser and Franck Bragigand. During the half-yearly flea market they have a stand where they offer their services. The public is invited to entrust them with objects bought at the flea market, so they can benefit from being transformed. During the following week they work in the publicly accessible workshop on redesigning the products submitted. At the end of the week the public picks up the 'new' things.

Fluid Functions

Another part of Open Borders is a project in the Carrefour hypermarket. Droog asks designer Cynthia Hathaway to select a number of Carrefour's sale items and to use simple handling techniques to transform them into new objects. The transformed products are exhibited at Carrefour with instructions for re-creating them yourself.

From Lille with Love

Gijs Bakker, Conny Groenewegen, Simon Heijdens, Chris Kabel, Wieki Somers, Paolo Ulian, Frederik Roijé, Arnout Visse, Marcel Wanders

As part of Open Borders, Droog Design develops various products in collaboration with regional industries: the glass giant ARC International in Arques, the ceramic industry Faiencerie d'Arc de Dèvres, lacemaker Desseilles Textiles SAS in Calais and optical fibres manufacturers Dubar-Warneton and Rubans Gallant in Roubaix.
The designers base themselves on existing product designs and add new elements to them, make combinations or new designs. One example is Wieki Somers' French Flemish glass, a combination of French wine and Flemish beer traditions.

Bar Europe

In honour of the Dutch Presidency of the EU, the Dutch Permanent Representation wants to offer a permanent gift to Europe. The Ministry of Foreign Affairs invites Droog Design to develop ideas for restyling the popular bar on the fifth floor of the Justus Lipsius Council building, the headquarters of the European Council in Brussels. Droog suggests incorporating a series of 25 chairs, one for each member state, and assigns Studios Müller and Van Tol the task of presenting an interior design with 'unity in diversity' as point of departure. The studios decide to leave the 'boring' framework as intact as possible, but to insert a number of elements to change the character of the space. The modular division of comfortable 'standard' chairs is playfully alternated with the EU chairs that can be moved anywhere in the bar. A special carpet is designed, composed of green surfaces and referring to nature and the geometric landscape of the Netherlands. The floor is inspired by the tiled floors of Dutch interiors of the Golden Age.

A clear distinction is made between the smoking and non-smoking area. In the smoking area voluminous ventilator hoods are decorated with landscapes in which light and sky are the principal features. These seventeenth and nineteenth century works by famous painters such as Johannes Vermeer and Jozef Israels look as if they are purifying the air and absorbing the smoke in the painted clouds. The non-smoking area is adorned with decorations modelled on seventeenth-century Dutch tulip vases and filled with artificial leafs that have been painted bright green by Franck Bragigand, as if to emphasize the healthy environment. At various points on the floor one can find specially designed meeting areas, the so-called Dutch Hangouts, which turn out to be perfect places for a brief chat. The concept of the ornate ventilator hoods is used for the meeting areas as well. In this case the hoods are covered with paintings by Johannes Vermeer. The Bar Europe opens on 1 September and is used every day by 4,500 people from 25 member states, employers and visitors of the building. The Ministry of Foreign Affairs describes the result of the refurbishing as follows: "For all the European civil servants the bar is a living room, away from home, an oasis in the EU building, a face in an anonymous environment."

First Class Executive lounge British Airways

British Airways is looking for a way to camouflage the enormous bulk of the air conditioning system in its first class lounge in London and asks Droog Design to think up a decorative solution. Designer Frank Tjepkema is awarded the commission and develops a tree form with decorative branches, which transports air from the ground to a higher level. Tjepkema's design is supervised by Droog Design in collaboration with Artiwise curators and wins first prize at the 2004 Dutch Design Awards in the interior category.

Nederlandse
Designprijzen
2004

Tijdens een prijsuitreiking in de Van Gendthallen in Amsterdam werden op 9 september de winnaars bekendgemaakt van de Nederlandse Designprijzen 2004. In totaal werden 15 prijzen toegekend, waaronder twee prijzen in de speciale categorie Design For All.

Binnen de 15 categorieën waarvoor ontwerpen konden worden ingezonden werden uiteindelijk 13 Nederlandse Designprijzen uitgereikt. Er waren in

Simply Droog, 10 + 1 years of creating innovation and discussion

Droog Design celebrates its 10 year anniversary with a travelling exhibition. Droog classifies its collection into 10 different themes it has addressed in the last 10 years: Reuse, Familiar/Not so familiar, Open design, The inevitable ornament, Simplicity, Irony, Tangibility, Experience, Hybridisation and Form follows process. Studio Jurgen Bey is asked to design the exhibition and comes up with a plan whereby the visitor is guided through fictitious living spaces. The 'apartments' are arranged on the basis of the 10 themes. The floor features two-dimensional rubber forms of attributes people use in daily life, such as a football or a bike. Besides the thematic part of the exhibition a historical survey is presented in a landscape of packing boxes, decorated with photographs, videos, drawings, models and publications.

Poster for Droog Design designed by children

The exhibition is launched in the Haus der Kunst in Munich in an impressive area of 1,600 m². In collaboration with the Premsela Foundation, the Haus der Kunst organises a special conference about Dutch design. The exhibition attracts about 25,000 visitors in 10 weeks. The exhibitor is received very well by the press. Chris Dercon, director of Haus der Kunst reports: "The public at large reacts particularly emotionally and formulates for itself, almost instinctively, the difference between Droog and the world of conventional design." The exhibition then travels to the Design Zentrum in Bremen, where it is on show for two months.

To accompany the exhibition a book is published covering the history of Droog's first eleven years in a nutshell.

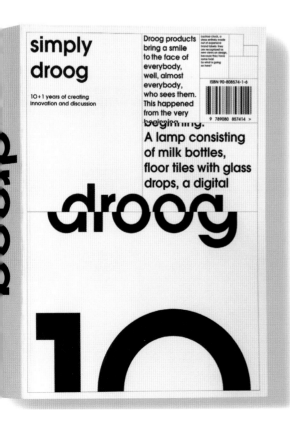

Droog Design is invited by the Gemeente-museum Den Haag to exhibit Simply Droog in The Hague for two months. Droog attaches great importance to the fact that the exhibition is also shown in its own country and gladly accepts the invitation. In collaboration with Studio Jurgen Bey, the exhibition is adapted to the Gemeentemuseum's spaces.

Opening droog@home

Droog Design moves into a splendid, historical building dating from 1641 at Staalstraat
7a-7b in Amsterdam. With an area of 700 m² the platform for contemporary design
at last has space to expand its activities. Droog Design's new building has a rich
historical background. It was the centre of the flourishing textile industry during those
days, housing the officials of the Amsterdam Drapers' Guild. Rembrandt painted his
masterpiece 'The Sampling Officials' especially for their board room. The office spaces
on the first and second floor were renovated in the Seventies and hardly deserve an
award for beauty. Nevertheless Droog Design leaves them just as they are found,
including radiators, kitchen units and ceiling lighting. The artist Franck Bragigand
covers everything from top to bottom in special colour combinations.
In renovating the 300m² large public space on the ground floor, Droog consults
Studios Müller and Van Tol. The idea is to regularly prepare meals for gatherings
and to organise informal meetings with designers in droog@home. Visitors can relax
and read in the 'library' and the space is furnished with products from the Droog
collection, which can be purchased on the spot. Many of the products are actually
used, for example the Tile Kitchen by Arnout Visser, Erik Jan Kwakkel and Peter van der
Jagt. The space is also used to display various exhibitions.

CASE
DA ABITARE

AMSTERDAM
- **I DROOG DESIGN
RIPARTONO DAL COLORE**
- **IL CARCERE DIVENTA
HOTEL DI TENDENZA**

**CITTÀ STAMPATE, FIORI,
GEOMETRIE OPTICAL,
FANTASIE, PATCHWORK**

**I TESSUTI CHE
CAMBIANO LA CASA**

**LETTI, COPERT
LENZUOLA
LE REGOLE
BUON DORM**

3 BUDGET 3 B

Christmas Design Dinner

Droog invites Richard Hutten, Jurgen Bey and Marcel Wanders, designers who have been involved with Droog Design since the beginning and are now all the rage, to organise an activity during the opening week of droog@home. They present a dinner for 50 people, prepared in the kitchen in the public space, at a dinner table mainly consisting of their own work (tables, chairs, plates) .

Droog BV

Droog BV is established in 2004. As a limited company Droog BV falls within the aims of Droog Design, but operates financially and organisationally completely independently of the foundation. Prototype designs emerge from Droog Design's experimental projects. If they have commercial potential these designs are developed further by Droog BV, taken into production and distributed. The new company also focuses on optimising the quality and lowering the price of classics from its collection.

Website

Droog launches its new website
www.droogdesign.nl. The website offers a lot
of information about Droog, the collection,
the projects, exhibitions and events, and offers
access to practically the entire Droog Design
archive. The website is 100% hypertext so
visitors can view the site in a playful and
associative way. The site has been developed
by Max Bruinsma, Thonik, in co-operation
with Shaun O'Neill, DMA.

Masterpieces

Eight young graduate students from the IM
course at the Design Academy in Eindhoven are
invited for an exhibition in droog@home: Jarrod
Beglinger, Marc Chataigner, Kuniko Maeda,
Ziv Marmur – CreACTion, Mario Minale, Itay Noy,
Tina Roeder and Roc Wang.

droog   ◀ ▶ • • •

droog | collection | projects | **publications** | education | news | press | contact | find
by droog | about droog

Publications

Right from the start, Droog has argued its curatorial outlook and
choices in texts which accompany presentations, projects and
exhibitions. A range of articles and a growing series of
catalogues and books by Droog's founders Renny Ramakers and
Gijs Bakker and by other authors connect the collection to its
cultural and professional contexts. As an active force in the
contemporary debate on design and product culture, Droog takes
position with provocative publications, both in terms of content
and form. The design of Droog's catalogues, for example, is as
much a statement on where we stand as the texts and products
contained in it. In that respect, Droog publications are as much
part of the collection of design products as the products are
published statements.

random image:

image: [Flexlamps by Sam Hecht in kitchen, 2005]

Publication page: 1 of 4 | Next

House Styling/Droog Design
17 Aug 2005 | ...

Wallpaper/The future of furniture
00 Jul 2005 | "For over a decade, maverick Dutch
design collective Droog, founded by design cr......

Icon/Milan top 10
00 Jun 2005 | "Nr. 3 droog was once again
responsible for the most thought-provoking show
in t......

Wallpaper/Dutch Masters
00 May 2005 | "The Netherlands announced its crack
at the presidency of the European Union las......

**Icon/Interview with Gijs Bakker
en Renny Ramakers**
00 May 2005 | "Yap! Ya ya. Yoo hoo. Bye!" That's
Gijs Bakker ending a call on his mobile phone......

Value for Money Checkbook
00 Apr 2005 | Value for Money Based on a concept
by: Niels van Eijk & Miriam van der Lubbe Exhibition
design......

Case da Abitare/Coloured Interiors
00 Jan 2005 | "A 17th century building in the heart
of Amsterdam has been transformed into a f......

sort results by: **date** ▾ | alphabet   show: 5 | 10 | 20 | all

2005

Presentation Milan, April 13–18

Value for Money
Ed Annink, Nick Armitage, Jan B., Niels van Eijk & Miriam van der Lubbe, Rody Graumans, Katja Gruijters, Martijn Hoogendijk, Eric Klarenbeek, Joris Laarman, Christien Meindertsma, Mario Minale, Ted Noten, orson+bodil, Roc Wang, Maurice Scheltens, Silvia van Schipstal, Frank Tjepkema, Susan Verheijen, Annelys de Vet, Marcel Wanders and Mina Wu.
Installation and initial concept: Niels van Eijk & Miriam van der Lubbe

Two different versions of the Chandelier 85 lamps: the original Chandelier 85 lamps features as a print on the Decorative Designer shade by Nick Armitage.

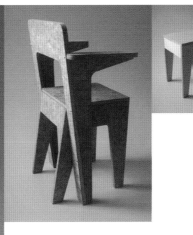

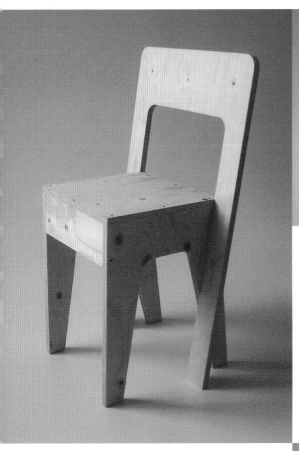

Value for Money

What determines the price of a product? Is it the amount of raw material or the value of the material? Is it defined by the production time, the labour costs, the edition or uniqueness? Or is it rather the reputation of the designer or brand that sets a product's price?

In Value for Money, Droog's 13th presentation in Milan, the visitor is invited to express his or her ideas on the criteria that determine the value of a product. The participating designers were asked to link the factors that determine the price to the factors that determine a product's emotional value, such as function, form, meaning, look, comfort, durability. More printing makes Maurice Scheltens' table-cloth more appropriate for more people. The stool by Niels van Eijk and Miriam van der Lubbe can be a chair or even an armchair for the same price when cheaper material is used. In the case of jewellery, emotional value and the value of the material often seem to coincide. Often it turns out that the final choice to pick a design is related to preferences in terms of price/quality ratio.

But what about the emotional value of the design? Does the consumer feel that this value is directly proportional to the product's price-determining value?

Three different stages of the stool by Niels van Eijk and Miriam van der Lubbe.

In Value for Money Droog displays the outcome of different stages of the production process and leaves the choice to the consumer. The visitors are challenged to give their opinion by attaching a filled in cheque from a specially designed chequebook to their preferred product. They thoroughly analyse their taste: the products valued most by the visitors often deviate from the products most expensive to produce.

T-shirt competition

Droog launches a T-shirt competition inviting all designers who wish to participate to send a concept for a short-sleeved T-shirt made of cotton. The number of entries is overwhelming: 354 contributions from over 40 countries are sent in. Droog selects a shortlist of nine winners. These designs are executed and are presented in gallery droog@home and on the website. One winning T-shirt is picked out of the short-list by public vote. 'The Tallest Man' by Sarah Dorkenwald and Ruth Spitzer (Canada) wins first prize, followed by 'A T-shirt should tell its own story' by Arlene Birt (U.S.A.) and 'Sweatshop-shirt ''do-it-yourself'' by Drus Dryden (New Zealand).

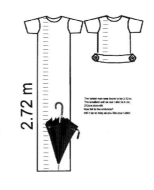

Travelling exhibition Simply Droog

After visiting Munich, Bremen and The Hague, the exhibition 'Simply Droog, 10 + 1 years of creating, innovation and discussion' continues its tour in Switzerland. The exhibition is hosted in former villas and is presented in two parts. Part one is located in the French speaking part of Switzerland: Lausanne (Mudac). Part two is located in the German speaking part of Switzerland: Zürich (Museum Bellerive). The Swiss railway company, SBB, provides special tickets to travel between both locations and see the whole exhibition. Simply Droog turns out to be a good way of connecting the two parts of Switzerland.

Following Switzerland, the exhibition is shown in the Museo Oscar Niemeyer in Curitiba, Brazil. The Droog exhibition takes over the whole surface-area of the gigantic 'eye' with which the building was extended a few years before. It looks like it has been made for the space. Whereas Simply Droog in Munich was mostly monumental and impressive, here the first impression is of beauty. All the 10 themes of the exhibition are presented in one oval space which gives a magnificent overview.

10. 12. 2005

Een plek om heel trots op te zijn

Museu Oscar Niemeyer
Museum Oscar Niemeyer
Curitiba - Paraná - Brasil

Groet Astrid

DROOG DESIGN
Renny Ramakers &
Gijs Bakker
Staalstraat 7a

1011JJ
Amsterdam
HOlanda

RPC

AKTUELLT DESIGN TRENDER MÄNNISKOR MOSAIK PRYLAR

sköna gröna sommardagar

Nu är det hög tid att luta sig tillbaka i solstolen, knappa in favoritkanalen på radion och njuta av högsommaren. Fäll upp parasollet när det är dags att smaka på sommarens primörer.

Årets finaste parasoll visade nederländska Droog Design på Milanomässan. Tyget är som löv och ger ett häftigt skuggspel.

En bärbar radio är ett måste för alla som inte vill missa sommarpratarna i P1. "Pal" i nya färgen lime, ca 2 000 kr, Tivoli Audio.

Fällbar vilstol av aluminium och polyestertyg är lätt att ta med till stranden, 298 kr, Plantagen.

REDAKTÖR SUSANNE HOVENÄS
MEDARBETARE MÄRTEN JANSON, ROGER NYSTRÖM, NINA SEDERHOLM

13

Droog BV

The first results of the development and production branch are presented under the Droog label, including Chris Kabel's Shadylace, created for the From Lille with Love project (2004), and Sam Hecht's Flexlamp.

Such den Schatten

Der nächste Hochsommer kommt (hoffe bestimmt. Dann kann endlich der roman Sonnenschirm seinen Auftritt haben, ein Ei

left FlexLamp for Droog
right Twice LCD alarm clock for Lexon
below right Solid range of knives for Taylor's Eye Witness
below Landscape camera, an experimental project that replaces the viewfinder with a mirror

Nº 13 Droog Design
Collective

BY AARON BETSKY

Droog changed everything. From its first exhibition at the furniture fair in Milan in 1993, the ragtag group of Dutch furniture, lighting, graphic, and product designers—who collaborate under the loose affiliation of what founders Gijs Bakker, a jewelry designer, and Renny Ramakers, a design critic, call "a brand and a mentality"—had begun to undermine the global design scene's steadfast allegiance to new looks and product innovation. With chairs made of piled-up secondhand clothing or rope dipped in resin, cupboards built of used wood, and crockery that looked broken or ill-formed, Droog created a cultural commentary about objects that heretofore had provoked few questions.

The International Design Magazine Our Power List Design's 40 Biggest Influencers plus Best Companies ... Living Legends ... Couples with Clout ... Design Divas

I.D.

The I.D. Forty
Who Drives Design?

Top of the List

Series on New Designers

droog@home starts a series of exhibitions featuring young design talents from different European countries. The exhibitions are completed with a fringe Open Talk programme and a dinner conceived by the exhibiting designers. Open Talk is meant to reflect on things in common, not on national differences. The designers discuss their approach to design, their sources of inspiration and their ideas on current developments in design. The first of this series is New Dutch Designers, presenting designers Wieki Somers, Simon Heijdens, Chris Kabel and Joris Laarman.

The second presentation in the series is New Swedish Designers, represented by the design group Front and featuring the first overview of their work. The press is most enthousiastic about the originality and humour in their designs. During their stay in the Netherlands, an Open Talk with the designers of Front is organised in droog@home and Jeroen Verhoeven from Demakersvan is invited to participate in the discussion as both designer groups just finished their studies very recently. The discussion deals with such topics as the role of random aspects in design, the meaning of design and the choice of working as a group.

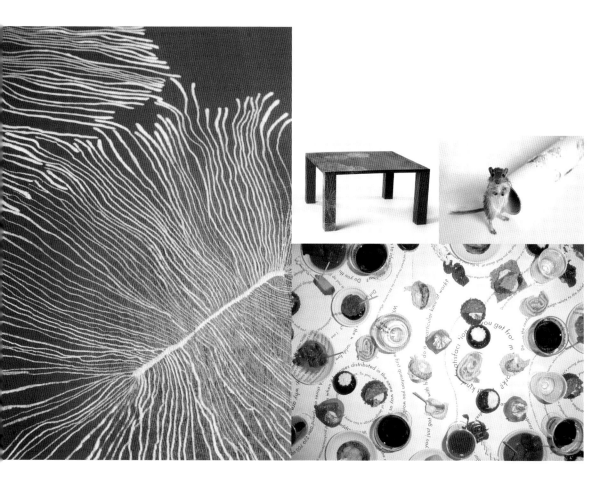

Urban Eco Diner for Nike

Nike brings a team from the United States over to Amsterdam, in order to have a better understanding of the European market and consumer. At Droog they have a 'brain picking' diner with Dutch creatives. Food designer Marije Vogelzang prepares an Urban Eco Dinner, playing along with Nike's recent focus on the ecological side of design.

Droog Dinner Delight

In December Droog organises an exclusive dinner event by food designer Marije Vogelzang, revolving around the theme of sharing. A special installation is made, with a table cloth going straight from the table up to the ceiling instead of hanging down from the table. The guests can put their arms and head through holes. Especially for this occasion Marije Vogelzang presents half plates, emphasizing the guests have to share their ingredients in order to create the perfect dish. Indeed a lively trade comes about at the dinner table. After an hour the first anarchist starts to tear the table cloth open to eat more comfortably and soon the others follow his example.

Dutch Prime Minister Balkenende has dinner at droog@home with representatives of the Dutch creative industry, in order to learn more about the sector, and is served a special selection of the menu card from the Slow Fast Food project.

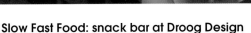

Slow Fast Food: snack bar at Droog Design

The 'slow' feeling from the Droog Design presentation during the Salone del Mobile 2004 in Milan is recalled in co-operation with the Slow Food organisation. For two weeks, Droog hosts a Slow Fast Food snack bar in its gallery droog@home. Products that you would traditionally find only in snack bars, such as hamburgers and chips, are prepared with ingredients based on quality, honesty and local availability and presented with subtle details like refined delicacies.

C.V.

1993

Milan	Droog Design

1994

Milan	Droog Design
Participation	Museum für angewandte Kunst, Köln, 'Design aus den Niederlanden'

1995

Milan	Droog Design by DMD
Solo exhibition	Kunsthal Rotterdam 'Droog Design'
Participation	Chapel Design Center, Köln, 'Droog Design & DMD'
	Museum Weserburg, Bremen, 'Die Kunst und das schöne Ding'
	Securitas Galerie, Bremen, 'Mentalitäten. Niederländisches Design'
	Caroussel du Louvre, Paris, 'Perigot Entreprises'
	MoMA , New York, 'Dutch coffee garden'
Fair DMD	Fiera Verona, 'Eco Way'

1996

Milan	Droog Design. Plastics new treat & Dry Tech + Droog Design by DMD
Project	Dry Tech
Participation	Gallery Andrea Leenarts, Köln, 'Droog Design'
	Centre du Design de l'Uquam, Montréal, 'Design Now! Design from the Netherlands'
	Übersee Museum, Bremen, 'Design im Wandel'
	Designzentrum, Stuttgart, 'Mentalitäten. Niederländiches Design'
	Museum of Modern Art, New York, 'Tresholds; Contemporary Design from the Netherlands'
	Material Innovation Gallery, New York, 'Material ConneXion'
	Sentou Galerie Paris 'Droog Design'

1997

Milan	Dry Bathing, new ideas for the bathroom + Dry Tech II, a new series of low-high-tech products / Droog Design for Rosenthal / Droog Design by DMD
Project	Dry Tech II
	Dry Bathing, new ideas for the bathroom
Commission	Droog Design for Rosenthal
Solo exhibition	Galerie im Pferdestall, Berlin, 'Droog Design. Zeitgenössisches Design aus den Niederlanden'

	Stilwerk Hamburg, 'Droog Design'
	Centraal Museum Utrecht, 'Droog Design'
Participation	Galerie Ulrich Fiedler, Köln, 'Droog Design'
	Gallery in Cork Street, London, 'Handmade in the Benelux'
	Victoria & Albert Museum, London, 'Not so simple'
	Taideteolissuusmuseo, Helsinki, 'Droog Design'
	Focke Museum, Bremen, 'Design mit Zukunft'
	Groninger Museum, Groningen, 'Mutant Materials in Contemporary Design'
Fair DMD	Fiera Milano International, 'Macev'
	Messe Frankfurt, 'Ambiente'
	Jacob K. Javits Convention Center, New York, 'Accent on Design'
	BEA Bern Expo, 'Ornaris'
	Messe Frankfurt, 'Droog Design for Rosenthal'
Lecture	Zaal De Unie, Rotterdam, 'Five years Droog Design'
Publication	'Droog Design 1991 - 1996' Centraal Museum Utrecht
Award	Prix d'Excellence de la Maison, Marie Claire
Purchase	Centraal Museum Utrecht purchases the Droog Design Collection

1998

Milan	The Inevitable Ornament
Project	The Inevitable Ornament
Solo exhibition	Murray Moss Store, New York, 'Eating potatoes with a silver fork'
Participation	Internationales Design Zentrum, Berlin, 'Sinn & Form'
	Taipei 'Dragon Fly'
	Stedelijk Museum Roermond, 'Droog Design 1991-1996, een begrip in de Nederlandse Vormgeving'
	San Francisco Museum of Modern Art, 'Do Normal: Recent Dutch Design'
	Alvar Aalto Museum, Jyväskylä, 'Empty?'
	Tel Aviv Museum of Art, 'Plastic Times'
	Verzameld Werk, Gent, 'Droog Design'
	La Mia Casa, Milano, 'Design on table'
	different locations in Europe, 'Materials in Design'
Fair DMD	Jacob K. Javits Convention Center, New York, 'Accent on Design'
	Messe Frankfurt, 'Tendence'
	Earls Court Two, London, '100% Design'
	Hallen Kortrijk, 'Interieur '98'
	Museum Waterland, Purmerend, 'Manifestatie Vormgeving'
Lecture	Design Galerie Wien, 'Symposium: Design as a marketing factor'
	Domus Academy, Milano, 'Droog Design'
	Jyväskylä, '2nd International Design for Architecture Symposium '
	Powerhouse Museum, Sydney, 'Droog Design'
Publication	'Spirit of the Nineties' 010 Publishers Rotterdam
Award	Dedalus Prize for European Design

1999

Milan	'Couleur Locale' Droog Design for Oranienbaum / 'A Touch of Glass' Droog Design for Salviati / 'Play House' An installation for Bang & Olufsen
Commission	'Couleur Locale' Droog Design for Oranienbaum
	'A Touch of Glass' Droog Design for Salviati
	'Play House' an installation for Bang & Olufsen
	'Data Treasures', a project for The New York Times Capsule Design Competition
	A logo for Documenta XI
	Personal Planner 2000 for WE
Solo exhibiton	Einzigart, Zürich, 'Einzigart zeigt Droog Design'
	Orangerie Schloss Oranienbaum, 'Couleur Locale'
	Jones, London, Droog + Levi's RED at Jones
Participation	SO/Joi'x Corporation Tokyo
	Pitti Imagine, Firenze, 'Materials in Design'
	Museum Louisiana, Copenhagen
	Galerie Intermezzo, Dordrecht
	Internationales Design Zentrum, Berlin, 'Stand der Dinge, International Design Yearbook Exhibition'
	Cyprus, 'Polytone'
	Museum Het Kruithuis, Den Bosch, 'Wanders Wonders'
	Vivid Designcenter, Rotterdam, 'Milaan in Rotterdam'
	Bilbao, 'Tapix'
	Centro Cultural de Belem, Lisboa, 'Double Dutch'
	Pitti Imagine, Firenze, 'By Hand'
	Murray Moss Store, New York, 'Opening of New Moss Store'
	Sydney, ICSID Congress Exhibition
	NWR Forum Kultur und Wirtschaft, Düsseldorf, 'Pluri Existenzen'
	Kunsthalle Krems, 'Haltbar bis… immer schneller'
	The Lighthouse, Glasgow, 'Identity Crisis'
Fair DMD	Messe Köln, 'Internationale Möbelmesse'
	Metro Toronto Convention Centre, 'Interior Design Show'
	Jacob K. Javits Convention Center, New York, 'Accent on Design'
	Fiera Milano International, 'Macev'
	Messe Frankfurt, 'Ambiente'
	Messe Basel, 'Ornaris'
	Messe Frankfurt, 'Tendence'
	Jaarbeurs Utrecht, 'Dutch Design Center'
	Earls Court Two, London, '100% Design'
	The Israel Trade Fairs & Convention Center, Tel Aviv, 'Habitat'
Lecture	Catena di Villorba, 'Droog Design at Fabrica'
	Berlage Instituut, Amsterdam
	Rice School of Architecture, Houston, 'Cullinan Chair'
Award	George Nelson Design Award
Publication	'Couleur Locale, Droog Design for Oranienbaum', 010 Publishers Rotterdam

2000

Milan	do + Droog Design = do Create / Indigo, Levi's RED Line
Project	do Create
Commission	Mandarina Duck Flagship Store Paris
	Window concept 'Indigo', Levi's RED Line
	Packaging for Levi's RED Line
	Fiera Milano International, 'Soft Bathroom'
Solo exhibition	Antique Boutique, New York, 'Indigo, Levi's RED Line'
	Jones, London, 'Indigo, Levi's RED Line'
	Colette, Paris, 'Indigo, Levi's RED Line'
	Colette, Tokyo, 'Indigo, Levi's RED Line'
	Israel Museum, Jerusalem, 'Droog Design'
	The Lighthouse, Glasgow, 'A private view of Droog Design'
	Institute for French Architecture, Paris, 'Droog Design Carte Blanche'
	US retail, Stockholm, 'Indigo, Levi's RED Line'
	Colette, Paris, 'do Create'
	Rocket Gallery, Tokyo, 'do Create'
	Sollentuna Exhibition Centre, Stockholm, 'Indigo, Levi's RED Line'
	different locations in the United States, 'Droog Design: Seven Year Retrospective'
	Kunsthal, Rotterdam, 'Droog Design + do = do Create'
Participation	Kunst Raum, Dornbirn, 'Haltbar bis … Immer schneller'
	Provinciehuis, Den Haag, 'Living Water Works'
	International Design Centre, Nagoya, 'Discover Holland, the Dutch new innovators'
	Techniekmuseum, Delft, 'What about Design'
	Café del Puerto, Bilbao, 'Indoméstico'
	Living Design Centre, Tokyo, 'Droog & Dutch Design'
	Vitra Design Museum, Berlin, 'Blow Up'
	Viaduct,London, 'The Great Outdoors'
Fair DMD	Messe Basel, 'Ornaris'
	Messe Köln, 'Internationale Möbelmesse'
	Messe Frankfurt, 'Ambiente'
	Jacob K. Javits Convention Center, New York, 'International Contemporary Furniture Fair'
	Jacob K. Javits Convention Center, New York, 'Accent on Design'
	Messe Frankfurt, 'Tendence'
	Earls Court Two, London, '100% Design'
	RAI, Amsterdam, 'Woonbeurs'
	Hallen Kortrijk, 'Biennale Interieur'
Lecture	Columbia University New York, 'Contrary Moves'
	University of Art and Design, Helsinki, 'Design World 2000'
	Konstakademiens, Stockholm, 'Droog Design'
	Lighthouse, Glasgow, 'Droog Design'
	Israel Museum, Jerusalem
	Institute of French Architecture, Paris, 'Salon d' Actualité'

	Harbourfront Centre, Toronto, 'Comfort: New Work from the Furniture Collective'
	Sollentuna Exhibition Centre, Stockholm
	Wolfsonian Museum, Miami
Publication	'Droog & Dutch Design', Centraal Museum Utrecht
	'do Create', Droog Design
	'Droog Design Catalogue' DMD & Droog Design
Award	Cologne Thumper
	Woonbeurs Pin
	Kho Liang Ie Prize
Purchase	Centraal Museum Utrecht purchases the Droog Design Collection

2001

Milan	'Me, Myself & You' / 'Pocket Furniture', Droog Design for Picus / Dry Kitchen
Project	Me, Myself & You, human contact in the 21st century
	Dry Kitchen
Commission	'Pocket Furniture', Droog Design for Picus
	Hybrid Highriser, Droog Design for Hoogstad Architecten
	'System Almighty' , Installation for 010101 Art in Technological Times, SF MOMA
	'Videorom', El Mundo Nuevo Valencia Biennial
	Packaging concept for Levi's RED Line
Solo exhibition	Architectural Association, London, 'do Create by Droog Design & do'
	Mandarina Duck Shop, Rue St. Honoré, Paris, 'Droog Design at Mandarina Duck'
	Trapholt Museum of Modern Art, Kolding, 'Droog Design`
	Teo Jacob Tagliabue, Genève, 'L'oeil écoute'
	Villa Noailles, Hyères, 'Villa Droog'
	Ecole Féderale Polytechnique, Lausanne, 'Droog Design 1993 - 2000'
	Kunsthal, Rotterdam, 'Me Myself & You + Dry Kitchen + Pocket Furniture'
Participation	San Francisco Museum of Modern Art, 'System Almighty'
	Maupertuus/Vos, Groningen, 'DMD en Droog Design'
	Societeit Baby, Amsterdam, 'Via Milano - New Dutch Design'
	Felissimo Design House, New York, 'Design 21'
	Salon Now, Paris, 'Vibration Européenne'
	EACC, Castelló, 'Un móvil en la patera'
	Kunsthalle Krems, 'Past Future Vision'
	Heineken Music Hall, Amsterdam, 'Tijdschriftenparade'
	Museum voor Moderne Kunst, Arnhem, 'Gelderse Vormgevingsprijs'
	Espace congrès de l'hôtel de ville, Roanne, 'Les Petits Papiers'
	different locations in The Netherlands, 'Reizende Galerie Energiezuinige Armaturen'
Fair DMD	Messe Köln, 'Internationale Möbelmesse'
	Metro Toronto Convention Centre, 'International Furniture Fair'
	Jacob K. Javits Convention Center, New York, 'Accent on Design'
	Messe Frankfurt, 'Ambiente'
	Jaarbeurs Utrecht, 'Dutch Design Center'
	The Apartment, Crosby Street, New York, 'Prospects'

	Jacob K. Javits Convention Center, New York,
	'International Contemporary Furniture Fair'
	The Jam Factory, London, '100% Design'
	RAI, Amsterdam, 'Woonbeurs'
Lecture	Architectural Association, London
	Luminaire, Chicago
	Potsdam 'Reden über Gestaltung'
	Jury Casa Brutus magazine, Tokyo
	Providence University, 'Droog Design'
Publication	DVD 'The real life of objects', The Lighthouse, Glasgow
	'Me, Myself & You', Droog Design
	'Pocket Furniture, Droog Design for Picus', Droog Design

2002

Milan	Real Life Revisited
Project	Hotel Droog´
	Restoring Daily Life
Commission	Tableau Vivant, Tableware for the Prefect of the Alsace
	Droog Design for Valli & Valli
	House & Home, Living in the 21st century, Abitare il Tempo Verona
	Window drops, retail concept for Levi's RED Line
Solo exhibition	Design Museum, London, The Conran Foundation 'Gijs and Renny go shopping'
Participation	The Crafts Council, London, 'Home Made Holland'
	Viaduct, London, 'Me, Myself & You'
	Musée de Design, Lausanne, 'Hide and Seek, Camouflage'
	Victoria & Albert Museum, London, 'Milan in a Van'
	Broel Museum, Kortrijk, 'Kunststof(f), Art & Design'
	Las Palmas, Rotterdam, 'Commitment, een keuze uit drie jaar FBKVB'
	Applied Arts Agency, London, 'Flat Pack'
	MARTa, Herford, 'Kunststof(f), Art & Design'
	Centraal Museum Utrecht, 'Ideaal ! Wonen'
droog & Co.	Reinventing Rituals, Michelle Huang
	Hotel Droog ★
	Tableau Vivant' Tableware for the Prefect of the area Alsace
	human=human, Franck Bragigand
	Redemption of the fake, Cynthia Hathaway
Fair TPM	Messe Frankfurt, 'Tendence'
Lecture	Contractworld, Hannover
	SCI-Art College, Los Angeles
	Museum of Contemporary Art, Houston
	Domus Academy, Milan
	Materials, Brugge
	Design Biennale, St. Etienne
	Roppongi Hills Information Centre, Tokyo
	Carnegie Mellon University, Pittsburgh

	Designers Association, Singapore
	Nederlands Architectuurinstituut, Rotterdam
Publication	'Less + More' 010 Publishers Rotterdam
	Video 'Hotel Droog', Droog Design
	'Hotel Droog', Droog Design

2003

Milan	Your Choice / Play-back / And…
Project	Your Choice
Commission	'Day Tripper', Streetscape Furniture Tokyo Mori Building
	Coffee shop 'Dutch Room' Premsela Foundation for Baltic House Theatre, St Petersburg
	Bless/Droog, Villa Noailles Hyères
Solo exhibition	Villa Noailles, Hyères 'Bless/Droog'
	Kunsthal, Rotterdam, 'Your Choice + Play-Back'
	Kulturhuset, Stockholm, 'Your Choice'
	Old Brewery Villa Holesovice, Praha, 'Your Choice'
	Seoul Arts Center, Seoul, 'No Design, No Style, Droog Design'
	Kyozon Gallery, Tokyo, 'Droog Design'
Participation	Nederlands Architectuurinstituut, Rotterdam, 'Reality machines'
	Galerie Sofie Lachaert, Tielrode, 'La table d'ouvrage'
	Studio Emiliana Design, Barcelona, 'Alehop!'
	Roppongi Hills, Tokyo, 'Roppongi Hills Public Art and Design'
	Applied Arts Agency, London, 'Go Dutch'
	Parc des expositions, Villepinte, Paris, 'Point d'eau'
	Design Museum, London, 'European Design Show'
	Centre de Cultura Contemporània de Barcelona, 'Creuats/Cruzados/Crossed'
	Musée de Préhistoire, Sauveterre La Lemance, 'Tournez design, aux origines du design'
droog & Co.	'The Placebo Project', Dunne & Raby
	Ronan & Erwan Bouroullec
	'Droog meets Bless'
Fair droog	RAI, Amsterdam, 'Via Milano 03'
	Messe Frankfurt, 'Tendence'
Lecture	Design Museum, London
	Design Laboratory Symposium, London
	IDSA National Conference, New York
	Kulturhuset, Stockholm
	Seoul Arts Centre, Seoul
	Craft Conference, Göteborg
	Designersblock, Tokyo
Publication	'Your Choice', Droog Design

2004

Milan	Go Slow
Project	Droog Event 1 'Open Borders'
Commission	'Bar Europe', European Council building Justus Lipsius for the Permanent Delegation of the Dutch Ministry of Foreign Affairs
	First Class Executive Lounch, London for British Airways
Solo exhibition	Kunsthal, Rotterdam, 'Go Slow' at foodfestival 'Rotterdam kookt'
	Tokyo Designers Block, Tokyo, 'Go Slow' in Tsumiki House
	Lille 2004, Lille, Droog Event 1 'Open Borders'
	Haus der Kunst, München, 'Simply Droog, 10+1 years of creating innovation and discussion'
	Design Zentrum, Bremen, 'Simply Droog, 10+1 years of creating innovation and discussion'
	Gemeentemuseum, The Hague, 'Simply Droog, 10+1 years of creating innovation and discussion'
Participation	Forum Universal de les Cultures 2004, Barcelona, 'Cubes of good ideas'
	Villa Noailles, Hyères, 'White Lights'
	Tri Postal, Lille 'Just what is it?'
	Musée de l'Hospice Comtesse, Lille 'Strangely Familiair, Design and Daily Life'
	Woonbeurs RAI, Amsterdam, 'Concrete Poetry' and 'Via Milano'
	Design Museum, Londen, 'Tank'
droog@home	'Masterpieces', eight international graduates IM masters
	Design Academy Eindhoven
	'Fluid Functions', Cynthia Hathaway
	Sandra Kassenaar
	'Christmas Design Dinner', Jurgen Bey, Richard Hutten, Marcel Wanders
Event	Victoria & Albert Museum, London, 'Go Slow' at Friday Late Night 'Consume this'
Lecture	Trapholt Museum of Modern Art, Kolding 'Concept and Beyond'
	Berlage Institute, Rotterdam 'Concept and Beyond'
Publication	Simply Droog, 10 + 1 years of creating innovation and discussion
	Design etc., Open Borders
	DVD Go Slow
	DVD Simply Droog

2005

Milan	Value for Money
	Photo shoot and presentation IO Donna
Project	Value for Money
	T-shirt Competition
Commission	Concept for 'Sony Vaio decoration'
	'Eventlab' for Volkswagen, Berlinale
	SHOWStudio 'Amaze Me'
Solo exhibition	Mudac, Lausanne, 'Simply Droog, 10+1 years of creating innovation and discussion'

	Museum Bellerive, Zürich, `Simply Droog, 10+1 years of creating innovation and discussion'
	Museo Oscar Niemeyer, Curitiba, `Simply Droog, 10+1 years of creating innovation and discussion'
Participation	Arcam Gallery, London, `Darkness'
	Design Academy, Paris, `Salon du Meuble Paris'
	Stadtmuseum Dusseldorf, Dusseldorf, `Play'
	Abitare@Schiferli showroom, Cologne and Milan, `Dolce Vita'
	Silvera furniture showroom, Paris, `Last exit to the Netherlands - Dutch affinities'
	Stedelijk Museum, Amsterdam, `NEST Gemeentelijke Kunstaankopen'
	Victoria & Albert Museum, London, `Touch Me'
	Woonbeurs, Amsterdam, `Via Milano'
	Kunstlicht, Eindhoven, `Design in Dialoog'
	Museum Waterland, Purmerend, `Nieuwe Nederlandse Vormgeving'
droog@home	`Simply Droog, 10+1 years of creating innovation and discussion: Irony'
	`Value for Money'
	`New Dutch Designers', Wieki Somers, Simon Heijdens, Chris Kabel, Joris Laarman
	`New Swedish Designers', Front
	`Urban Eco Dinner', Marije Vogelzang
	`Slow Fast Food: snack bar at Droog Design', Slow Food
	`Droog Dinner Delight', Marije Vogelzang
Lecture	Hong Kong Arts Centre, `What's good' Hong Kong
	Centro Cultural de Belèm, `Experimenta Design 2005', Lisbon, What's the message?
	Istanbul Design Week, `Design Meet', Istanbul, `Concept and Beyond'
	Universidad Iberoamericana, `MX Design Conference', Mexico City, `Concept and Beyond'
	Gwangju Design Biennale, Gwangju, `Five senses for this millennium'
	Inspirational Design Happening, Milan
Publication	Value for Money cheque book

photo index

Products

Designers

credits

Editor Renny Ramakers (first edition), Anneke Moors (second edition)

Texts Aaron Betsky, Ole Bouman, Ed van Hinte, Ellen Lupton, Louise Schouwenberg, Marieke Sonneveld, Jaakko van 't Spijker

Assistant Astrid Honold

Documentation Chawwah Six

Translation into English Michael Gibbs

Photography Gijs Bakker, Rien Bazen, F. Bouguet, Maurice Boyer, Henri Brekveld, Max Bruinsma, Erica Calvi, Feddow Claassen, Fendry Ekel, Allard Faas, Bob Goedewagen, Dini Hillebrand, Cathrine von Hauswolff, Thea van den Heuvel, Astrid Honold, Lucy Huiskens, Katja K, Mischa Keizer, Ron van Keulen, Christoph Kicherer for Domus Magazine, Alexey Kompaniichenko, Rene Koster, Jannes Linders, Tor Lindstrand, Marsel Loermans, Elise van der Mark, Hans van der Mars, Anneke Moors, Ernst Moritz, Bianca Pilet, Inga Powilleit, Uwe Quilitzsch, Monica Ragazzini, Renny Ramakers, Joke Robaart, Misha de Ridder, Maurice Scheltens, Bruno Scotti, Rik Seisveld, Nienke Terpstra and the designers

Special credits to models James, Rene, Jos Wittebol, Tessel Peijenburg, Bob Flake (Fotoformation)

Design Thonik

Printed by Drukkerij Onkenhout BV, Hilversum

Lithography Frits Repro, Drukkerij Onkenhout BV

Publisher Droog, Amsterdam/ www.droogdesign.nl

Copyright © 2006 the authors and Droog

ISBN 90-808574-2-4